# Conspiracy of Silence

**Pastor
Ron Vietti**

# Conspiracy
## of Silence

**Pastor
Ron Vietti**

SIMPLE LIFE

Scripture quotations, unless noted, are taken from the New American Standard Bible®, copyright © 1960, 1962, 1967, 1968, 1971, 1972, 1973, 1975, 1977, 1995 by The Lockman Foundation. Used by permission. (www.lockman.org)

First Edition

Cover Illustration: Scott Garcia
Design by Ragont Design

Library of Congress Control Number: 2002111177
ISBN: 0-9721-7680-2

# ACKNOWLEDGEMENTS

This book would not be possible without God's gracious patience with me. Many times over again, I have tested His Spirit with my stubborn ways—yet He has been kind and gracious to me. I will forever appreciate His loving kindness and longsuffering character.

I would also like to express my deepest thanks to Kelly Johnston in Colorado Springs, Colorado, for keeping me on the straight and narrow way and correcting my redneck grammar. I also want to thank my daughter Tara Crews for the long hours she spent taking care of the details—without her, this book would not have been written. Thanks to Josh for just being my son. Last, but not least, I owe a big thank-you to my wife for sticking with me and loving me considering all the challenges I have put her through.

# TABLE OF CONTENTS

# FOREWORD

A conspiracy exists to destroy all of the Christians on the face of the earth. Very few people are aware of what it is or how it works, much less that it exists.

Webster's Dictionary defines conspiracy as "a combination of persons for an evil purpose, a plot." Christians have a common enemy referred to in the Bible as Satan, Lucifer or the Devil, and his cohorts are often called demons or spirits of darkness. It is their job to see to it that the Church is rendered ineffective in its dealings with the world, as well as kept in a constant state of defeat and turmoil so Christians will never have the time nor the energy to effectively bring the light of God's love and the knowledge of His Kingdom to a hopelessly lost world. Unfortunately, they are doing a superb job! The people of God need to begin to recognize that spiritual entities are daily trespassing into our personal lives in order to blind us to the truth. God's Word is the truth. God has explained to us in His Word that all of us from the fall of Adam are genetically coded with sin. You might say that we are sick with a terminal illness. If left alone in this depraved condition, we will die. Satan has more than adequately blinded the world to this truth. He has used the movie media, music industry, as well as the higher academic institutions to make us believe that this whole idea of man's depravity is at best a moronic joke. He has blinded the unbeliever's eyes. In 2 Corinthians 4:3-4, we are told: "And even if our gospel is veiled, it is veiled to those who are perishing, in whose case the god of this world has blinded the minds of the unbelieving that they might not see the light of the gospel of the glory of Christ, who is the image of God." God's spiritual prescription for the unsaved is to receive the Holy Spirit and be saved from their sins. If they allow the world, through its various venues, to keep them blinded from the truth of the gospel of salvation, they will most assuredly experience the death of their souls as spoken of in the Bible. Once they die they will be faced with the judgment of God, and though they may realize they've been blinded to the truth, it will be too late to do anything about it. The demons of this world have successfully kept them blinded to the truth of the gospel, and that, in my opinion, is a very evil thing to do.

Not only has God written out a spiritual prescription for nonbelievers, He has also written out a spiritual prescription for believers. In order to keep us healthy, He has given us such words as: "Abide in Me, and I in you. As the branch cannot bear fruit of itself, unless it abides in the vine, so neither can you, unless you abide in Me. I am the vine, you are the branches; He who abides in Me, and I in him, he bears much fruit; for apart from Me you can do nothing" (John 15:4-5). For us Christians, our prescription reads: Daily abide in the

Lord, His Word and presence in order to keep the sin nature in a state of remission. Failure to do so will cause the sin nature to become active in our lives again. It's imperative that we understand that we must pray and meditate on Scripture daily, and fellowship with other believers in order to keep spiritual life flowing in our lives. The Bible explicitly teaches this truth over and over in various portions of Scripture, yet the devil has successfully intruded into Christians' lives with his lies, overly busy schedules and distractions, to such a degree that we have been disobedient to this "abiding" principle. I believe this is all a part of an evil conspiracy by a committed demonic realm to keep the average Christian in a state of defeat and, at the same time, unable to evangelize the lost. It should seem obvious to us all that if our schedules don't change and our habits aren't reevaluated, then the world will never be won for Christ. It takes both time and energy to keep us healthy and to evangelize the lost. I believe we have become victims of a conspiracy. Again, I must tell you that Ephesians 6:12 breathes the inspirational, infallible word of God when it says: "Our battle is not against flesh and blood, but against people without bodies." LB

The majority of us Christians have no idea how God expects us to live or the wonderful outcome of God's response to the people who dare to delve deeper into the things of the spirit world. A new world is opened up to people who treat angels and demons as real entities, and expect God to openly communicate with them daily. Most of us live in a state of spiritual ignorance, oblivious to the war going on around us every day. Bombs explode in the workplace, people are gunned down in the church, including the pulpit. And somehow, we have watched this happen without making the spiritual connection to all the chaos and devastation. I believe with all my heart that God wants the church to wake up, wipe off the dust from our spiritual weapons, and recommit ourselves to the war at hand. We need warring soldiers in the body of Christ today—men and women who are not afraid to fire a weapon; who refuse to retreat or give up any ground to the enemy. We need Christian soldiers who will not stand by any longer and watch the spiritual devastation continue in our churches and communities without launching a counter-attack. We need to have the Holy Spirit open our eyes to see the spiritual connection to the bloody trails left on our side-walks as we leave our homes to go to work. We must not stand by idly on the sidelines and erroneously buy into the lie that Satan is not directly behind all the chaos. We must not be so naïve to think that he has nothing to do with the programming that comes through our television sets or the music our children listen to. Ephesians 2:2 says that Satan is the "prince of the power of the air." In 1 John 5:19 it says, "We know that we are of God, and the *whole world* lies in the power of the evil one" (italics mine). Now either we believe that or we don't.

I am convinced that it's our duty to inform our bleeding neighbors of the truths of the gospel, because if they understood these truths, life would be totally different for them. The God of the universe has revealed these truths to us so we would live sensibly and not be hurt. If the Church really believed the Word of God the way we boast we do, then we would do things a lot differently than we are doing them now. If we really believed what Ephesians 2:2 and I John 5:19 says, then we would not stand by for one more moment and allow our television programming to go unmonitored or let our children bring home whatever they wished from the music stores without some sort of strict scrutinizing.

The Devil and his demons are very much alive and active in the world today. There is hardly an area of society that Satan has not invaded and corrupted, to some degree. Yet, for the most part, the Church has failed to recognize this profound truth. We live as though the Devil doesn't exist, or we wrongly conclude that his demons and power are not like the Bible has made them out to be. Something has to change. Things cannot remain as they are. We cannot allow the Devil's domain to go on being uncontested. He is being given way too much freedom to move around and do all he wishes.

One intention of this book is to unveil some of the truths and untruths about the spiritual domain. It is my desire, as well as I believe the Holy Spirit's, to awaken every person who reads this book to the realization that God wants a *personal* relationship with him or her. It's only through a personal walk with Him each and every day that we'll be able to counteract the onslaught of demonic destruction. God has always wanted to have a personal relationship with His people since the beginning of time, and why we would even perceive that the entire personality and workings of God have changed is totally beyond me. For example, in the Old Testament, God walked daily with Adam and Eve in the Garden. Apparently, the relationship was personal and intimate. Then, Adam and Eve moved away from God through sin and disobedience, but that didn't stop God. A few years later, He located a guy by the name of Abraham, who had an open heart toward Him. God walked closely with him until Abraham died. Throughout the Old Testament, God demonstrates His desire to talk to and lead His people in a variety of ways, whether it is through a burning bush, a spiritual dream or vision, angelic visitations, or through the means of a prophet or priest who would visit someone and give them a word in God's Name. God has always wanted to be a personal, intimate God to His people, but somewhere along the way, many of us have failed to take advantage of His loving offer and extended grace. The result is misery and suffering.

The primary intention and purpose of this book is to inspire in God's people a passion to walk with Him in a more intimate way. This book will offer some very practical insights that will help Christians recapture this personal walk with God. Our adversary the Devil has been trying to hide these truths from God's people throughout the ages. It's all a part of the conspiracy.

# 1

# ANGELS ARE AMONG US
❖

*"I do not know how to explain it: I cannot tell how
it is. But I believe angels have a great deal to do
with the business of this world."*

—◦ CHARLES H. SPURGEON [1] ◦—

*"The angels are near to us. They have long arms,
and although they stand before the face and in the
presence of God and His Son Christ, they are hard
by and about us in those affairs which by God we
are commanded to take in hand."*

—◦ MARTIN LUTHER [2] ◦—

On a Friday night in December, Joshua, my twenty-one-year old son, told me he was going up to Mountain High Ski Resort the next morning to do some snowboarding. I didn't feel good about this particular trip, so at 5:30 Saturday morning, when I heard him leave the house, I prayed a simple, but impactful prayer: "Lord, please send an angel with Joshua today, and cause that angel to do whatever is necessary to keep him from any serious harm. If he gets into any trouble, cause the angel to manifest himself and help him. In Jesus' Name I pray, amen." Now that's basically all I prayed, before I rolled over and went back to sleep.

I woke up a couple hours later and went about my normal routine, getting prepared for Sunday's sermon. Almost four thousand people would be assembled together at the church I had pioneered almost twenty-eight years ago, Valley Bible Fellowship in Bakersfield, California. At 3:30 in the afternoon, I went to the bedroom to take a quick one-hour power nap. I figured that Joshua would probably be in late that night. Since I was a light sleeper, and he would most assuredly wake me up when he came in, I figured I could use the nap.

I had not quite fallen asleep when my wife awakened me. She said, "Ron, Mike just called, and Joshua has been in a bad snowboarding accident. An ambulance has been called to the ski resort, and they are going to take him to a hospital in San Bernardino. They think he has broken his hip." I got up, and got dressed, and then Debbie and I jumped in our car and began the two-hour drive to San Bernardino. Immediately we began to pray that God would minister to Josh in his pain and give the hospital staff a spirit of wisdom as they examined him. As we prayed, we were both completely bathed in a spirit of peace and confidence that everything was going to be okay. When we arrived at the hospital, we were greeted in the waiting room by six of Joshua's friends—still wearing their ski gear. They had kindly stayed by his side the whole time. Josh was heavily sedated when we arrived and, much to our relief, the nurse told us that his hip had been dislocated, not broken. We were told Josh could go home as soon as the sedative wore off and the doctor released him. I think we got back in Bakersfield sometime Sunday morning. I had time for a quick three-hour catnap before putting the finishing touches on my sermon.

Nearly two days later, Beth, one of Josh's friends who accompanied him on his trip, told us about something that had happened on the slopes the day of Josh's accident. What she said confirmed our belief in the presence of angels among us.

According to Beth, when the group received news that Joshua had been hurt, she and some of the others decided to wait at the bottom of the hill. As the ski patrol descended with Joshua, a skier dressed in black snowboard pants, a black sweatshirt and a stocking cap followed them. Beth and Josh's friends followed the ski patrol to the medical building, as did the mystery skier. He appeared to be about seventeen years old, and he obviously wasn't with the ski patrol. *Who is he?* Beth wondered. The skier sat in a chair that was fairly close to Joshua, fixing his gaze on Joshua. As soon as the medical staff lifted Josh onto the examining table, they insisted everyone leave the room. Everyone complied except the mystery skier. Beth thought, *Why is he allowed to stay in the room, when everyone else has to leave?*

After awhile, Beth went back into the room to ask the staff where Josh would be taken so she could inform us of his whereabouts once we arrived. As she entered the room, a new emergency attendant, who had just come on shift, asked the other attendant if anyone had witnessed the accident. The skier stood and said that he had witnessed the whole thing. He commenced to give them a detailed account. He acted as if he were Josh's best friend, so Beth tried to get close to the young man to ask him who he was and how he knew Josh. But no matter how hard she tried, the young man would not make eye contact with her nor would he acknowledge her presence in the room. He just focused on Josh. When the staff again asked everyone to leave the room, everyone did, except the skier, who the staff seemed to ignore.

After some more time passed, Beth went back into the room to ask the staff another question. As she entered, she heard Josh cry out, "My leg! My leg! It really hurts!"

As he spoke those words, the skier walked over to Joshua's bed, gently slipped his hands under Joshua's right knee, and cradled Joshua's leg. The emergency tech, who acted as if she didn't see the young man, walked over and began moving Joshua's foot around, trying to alleviate some of the pain.

Josh told her, "It's my leg, not my foot!" The young man continued to hold Joshua's leg, and the pain subsided. Again, Beth was asked to leave, and again, the young man was ignored.

As she left the room Beth wondered, *Why in the world are they letting that young man touch Josh? They act oblivious to his presence.*

After the ambulance arrived, and Josh was transferred into it for the ride to the hospital in San Bernardino, the skier dressed in black disappeared. Later, Beth asked Mike, another member of the group, what he thought about the young man in the room. Mike replied, "What young man?" Now Mike had been in the room as often as Beth, but he claimed he never saw the skier dressed in black.

When Beth told Mindy, one of the other girls in the group there, about the strange occurrence, Mindy remarked, "Maybe it was an angel."

When Beth told the story to her mother, her mother suggested she share the story with us. But Beth wasn't sure. She later told me that she didn't want to be embarrassed. After all, what if this guy was a close friend of Joshua's and he just didn't tell anyone? She had not yet had an occasion to speak with

Josh after the accident, so she began to pray, "God, if this was an angel, please confirm it to me before I go to Pastor Ron and Debbie." As she prayed, she said that a desire came into her heart to pick up her Bible. She prayed God would supernaturally cause her to turn to a passage that would either confirm or dismiss her convictions that this could very well have been an angel from God. "Just give me a verse with the word 'angel' in it," she said. She flipped open her Bible, which opened to the book of Galatians, chapter four. Her eyes focused on verse fourteen: "And that which was a trial to you in my bodily condition you did not despise or loathe, but you received me as an *angel* of God, as Christ Jesus Himself"(italics mine). There it was—the word "angel."

Her story left me anxious to talk with Joshua. After I told him the whole story, he was amazed. He insisted there was no one on the hill when he had his accident. "In fact," he said, "I was in a snowboard park, and there were absolutely no skiers or snowboarders in the vicinity at that time."

I asked him if he was coherent the whole time he was being treated at the ski resort, and he told me that he was. Then I asked him, "If someone had been sitting in the room with you, just a few feet from your right side for almost an hour and a half, would you have been aware of his presence?"

"Dad, I absolutely would have known if someone had been sitting in the room with me. There was no one in that room with me except the emergency tech, and at no time did any young boy or anyone else approach the bed and hold my leg up in the air. I was carefully watching who touched me, and the young man you described did not exist."

I knew right then and there I had an angel story to tell on Christmas Sunday.

In my twenty-eight years of ministry I have read a lot of stories about angels. In many of these stories I have found two things to be true: First of all, most of the angels people have seen manifest themselves as young men. Second, they usually have blue eyes. I couldn't verify the color of eyes this young man had because Beth said he hadn't looked at her, only Joshua. According to Hebrews 13:2, we are not to "neglect to show hospitality to strangers, for by this some have entertained angels *without knowing it*" (italics mine). Hebrews 1:14 says, "Are they not all ministering spirits sent out to render service for the sake of those who will inherit salvation?" Throughout the Bible, men and women of God had angelic visitations—Abraham and his wife Sarah, Lot, Jacob, Moses, Balaam, a group of Israelites in Judges chapter two, Gideon, David, Elijah, Ornan, Daniel, Zechariah, Joseph, Mary Magdalene, Mary the mother of Jesus, Zacharias, a group of shepherds, some of the apostles in Acts 5, Phillip, Cornelius, Paul and Peter. All of these people had angelic visitations. Psalm 34:7 says the Angel of the Lord encamps around those who fear Him.

Our enemy, the devil, does not want God's people to know about the reality of angels. He thrives on placing fear in our hearts. For example, I worry a lot about my kids when they are not at home. My wife doesn't worry nearly as much as I do, unless I infect her with my fears. Worry and fearful living creates havoc in our fellowship with God. It's hard to be connected to what God is doing in our lives if we give into worry. Fear makes us ineffective conduits for ministry. When we become consumed with worry, our ability to give others the Holy Spirit's counsel and encouragement becomes diminished. Philippians 4:6 commands us to be anxious for nothing, but to make our requests known to God. It says, "Don't worry, but pray!" If we don't pray, maybe we *should* worry. The Bible puts prayer in the place of worry. Philippians goes on to say that if we pray and don't worry, God will give us a peace that passes understanding. And that peace, it says, will guard our hearts and our minds. As I look back in my life, I see many examples of how I made some stupid decisions simply because I was anxious about something. Had I prayed and submitted my requests to God, I would have had a peace in my life that would have kept me from doing these stupid things. My life would be different today if I had truly believed in God and His provision when I prayed.

If we believe not only in the existence of angels, but also firmly in their ability to help us in times of need, then our worry quotient can be considerably lowered. Not a day goes by that I don't start out by asking God to send angels with my kids and wife wherever they go. I put trust in that prayer, and I thank God for hearing it. Then the rest of the day I rest, knowing God's angels are close at hand to help protect my family. Then and only then can I be free to take care of God's business. Jesus once said, "Be it done to you according to your faith" (Matthew 9:29). I believe in angels and what the Bible has to say about them.

When angels become active in our lives, they are not always seen by the naked eye. When the angel of God stood in the path of Balaam in Numbers 22, the angel was invisible, seen only by the donkey, until God in His divine sovereignty, opened the eyes of Balaam.

In John 5, we are told about an angel from God who came down to the pool of Bethesda in Jerusalem at certain seasons and stirred up the water. Whoever was the first to step into the water was healed from whatever infirmity plagued him or her. Whether this was a real event or a myth, the idea that the angel remained in the spiritual realm and was invisible to the people made him no more or less active in their midst. I'm positive that Psalm 34:7 is true when it says, "The angel of the Lord encamps around those who fear Him." That means that an angel encamps around me. However, I have never visibly seen that angel.

When my daughter, Tara, was two years old, we were at a relative's apartment complex for lunch. They had a pool at the apartment complex, and before lunch we decided to take a swim. While I soaked up some rays, my wife and mother-in-law watched Tara. They let her wade around on the steps of the pool. We are what you would probably call an over-protective family. We watch our kids really well. I had been lying by the pool half asleep for about thirty minutes when all of a sudden I felt as though someone had shaken me and said, "Look for your daughter!" That's the best way I can describe it. It was such a dramatic awakening that I sat straight up, startled. I looked around and saw my wife and mother-in-law sitting at the other end of the pool visiting, and that gave me the assurance that everything was okay. Surely they knew where Tara was. So I lay back down on the lounger, closed my eyes and tried to go back into my restful state. But once again I felt my spirit roused. I sat up and looked around the pool for my daughter but didn't see her. I was about to lay back down again when my eyes caught a glimpse of a small body at the bottom of the pool. Tara! I dove into the pool and grabbed the lifeless body. When I surfaced, I prayed, "Oh God, help me!" I repeated that phrase three or four times, and each time she spat up a mouthful of water. After about thirty seconds, she pushed me away. When I put her on the sidewalk, she began to walk around the pool singing, "God is so good"—a bit unusual for a nearly drowned two-year-old, I thought. For years I have rehashed this incident in my mind. Who shook me out of my sleep and told me to look for my daughter? The best explanation I can come up with is that an invisible angelic being caused the concern.

In Hebrews we're told that angels are "ministering spirits, sent out to render service for the sake of those who will inherit salvation" (1:14). Angels are spirits who can affect our lives. The more we become acquainted with angels, the more effective we can be in the Kingdom of God. We must come to the place where we live in such a way that we never write off anything as mere coincidence. "Therefore, gird your minds for action, keep sober in the spirit" (1 Peter 1:13a). The Christian life, properly lived, should be one of action.

A few years ago, my wife and I drove to a nearby park to have some pictures made. For some reason, I decided to carry my pager—something I rarely do. At that time there were only two people, besides my wife, who knew my pager number—my son and daughter.

When my wife and I arrived at the park, I took my pager off of my belt clip and threw it in the backseat. When we were through taking pictures, we went back to the car to go home. As soon as I sat down in the car, my pager went off. I concluded right away that it must be Josh or Tara. But the number that flashed on my pager was one I didn't recognize. I reached for my cell phone, and my wife said, "You're not going to call them back, are you? You know it's a wrong number."

But I was curious, so I decided to dial the number. A woman picked up the phone. I introduced myself as Ron Vietti, and said, "You just paged me, so I'm returning the call."

"I didn't page anyone," she replied. "How did you get my number?" she asked.

I explained that her number had appeared on my pager screen, but she insisted she hadn't called me.

Regardless, I wasn't ready to let her off of the hook. "Let me at least pray with you," I pled.

"Okay, go ahead, but make it quick," she said.

So I prayed something like: "Oh Lord, I don't know why this lady's phone number appeared on my pager or why my pager went off. Only You know why. But I ask You today to bless her in all areas of her life and let her see just how much You love her. And God, whatever she's going through, be with her."

Then I did what I felt the Holy Spirit wanted me to do. I began to take authority over a spirit of depression, discouragement and even suicide. At the time, I had no idea as to why I was doing this, but as I took authority over the spirit of suicide repetitiously, the lady began to weep uncontrollably and yell at me, "Why did you call me? Who gave you my number? I didn't page you!"

I replied, "I know you didn't page me. You couldn't have even if you wanted to. I have an unlisted number." But curiosity welled up inside me. "Tell me, what's going on?" I said.

Between sobs, she opened up and told me something that put chill bumps on my chill bumps. She said, "I decided to kill myself today. I have already written my suicide note and have all the stuff lying on the couch to do it. And that's when you called. In the next hour, it would have been all over. I can't understand how you knew or why you called."

"I guess an angel paged me," I answered. I gave her some counsel and prayed with her until she convinced me she would not kill herself.

I'm convinced angels were involved. My life is not boring to say the least, but then again, I believe in angels. I believe in miracles, and I believe that God wants my life to be full of action. I see many Christians rotting in a state of boredom, because they have fallen prey to Satan's conspiracy to keep us ignorant of and blind to angels and the supernatural realm. He knows that if our eyes are ever opened, the boring things of this old world will lose their value, and we will become valuable conduits for God in this world.

1. Charles Haddon Spurgeon, *Spurgeon's Sermons, Vol. 2* (Grand Rapids: Baker Book House, 1983), 191.

2. Martin Luther, *The Table Talk of Martin Luther,* Ed. Thomas S. Kepler (Grand Rapids: Baker, 1952), 279-280.

# DEMONS—
# THESE GHOSTS ARE FOR REAL

❖

*"There are two equal and opposite errors into
which our race can fall about the devils. One is to
disbelieve in their existence, the other is to believe
and to feel an unhealthy interest in them."*

—ᴏ C. S. LEWIS ᴏ—

*"Millions of unseen creatures walk the earth,
unseen both when we wake and when we sleep."*

—ᴏ JOHN MILTON IN *PARADISE LOST* ᴏ—

No educated person in his right mind would believe in demons, right? Wrong! It's the uneducated mind that doesn't believe in the existence of demons. God, the most intelligent being in the universe, believes in demons. In fact, in the beginning, He created them, not as demons but as angels. Ephesians 6:12 says, "For our struggle is not against flesh and blood, but against the *rulers,* against the *powers,* against the *world forces of this darkness,* against *the spiritual forces of wickedness in the heavenly places*" (italics mine).

I ascribe to the theory most commonly called the "gap theory." In its most elementary form, the gap theory teaches us that there were pre-Adamic (before the time of Adam) beings on this earth. This theory is based on two premises. The first premise comes from Genesis 1:28, where God tells the man (Adam) to go forth and "replenish" the earth. One of the meanings of replenish is "to go do it over again." In fact, this is the same word God uses when He tells Noah, in Genesis 9:1, to go out and *repopulate* the earth. Therefore this seems to indicate the existence of pre-Adamic beings. The second premise for the gap theory stems from the gap between the creation account in Genesis 1:1 and the text found in Genesis 1:2. According to Genesis 1:1, God created a perfect world but, in the gap between verses one and two, something happened that made Him void His creation and basically start all over: "In the beginning God created the heavens and the earth. And the earth was formless and void, and darkness was over the surface of the deep; and the Spirit of God was moving over the surface of the waters."

The key question is: What happened to make God that angry at the world? One possibility is that Lucifer was cast out of heaven during this gap period, and when he came to the earth, he corrupted the pre-Adamic beings. Isaiah 14:17, speaking of the fall of Satan, describes him as one "who made the world like a wilderness and overthrew its cities, who did not allow his prisoners to go home."

I realize there are many who reject this theory, and that's okay, because it won't take away from what I am going to say in the rest of this chapter. Some will say that this particular verse doesn't speak of Satan at all, but Nebuchadnezzar or Sennacherib. Nonetheless, this theory is food for thought because those who hold to it could conclude that these pre-Adamic beings were wiped out between verses one and two by the Flood. Therefore they lost their physical bodies to death, but Lucifer kept their spirits with him, and they became the part of the demonic host referred to by Paul as "the world forces of darkness" (Ephesians 6:12).

These pre-Adamic spirits, who once had bodies, are the spirits who possess human bodies when given the opportunity. They miss their old bodies, and the only way they can enjoy the lusts of this world is by occupying an earthly suit. So, at every opportunity, they possess a body and party down. People have to do some pretty wicked stuff to put themselves in a place where a demon can enter a body, but it does happen.

The New Age Movement utilizes people called "channelers." These individuals are said to be gifted people who have learned how to channel spirit guides. There are many people in the United States who claim to have become channelers for what they believe to be "divine spirit guides from another time and era." People pay a lot of money to hear these spirit guides speak through these individuals. I once had the opportunity to view one of these channelers in action. He called on his spirit guide to come. Then he made all sorts of faces and gestures as the spirit guide made his presence known in the channeler's body. He allowed the spirit guide to speak through him using his vocal chords and body to relay his message to the audience. I suggest this is a revelation of a demon that has invaded and lives in the body of the channeler.

In Revelation 12:4 we learn that "[the dragon's] tail swept away a third of the stars of heaven, and threw them to the earth." Many Bible scholars believe this verse speaks of the one-third of the angelic host who were cast out of heaven with Lucifer at his fall. This belief is also common according to Jewish tradition. If this is true, then these angels would represent the division of demons referred to in Ephesians

6:12 as the "spiritual forces of wickedness in the heavenly places." These would be the ruler demons that never possess bodies, but have authority over cities, countries and municipalities.

There are many references to ruler demons as being "princes." For example, Daniel 10:13 speaks of the prince of Persia, and Ezekiel 21:25 refers to the wicked one—the prince of Israel. The prince of Rosh is identified in Ezekiel 38:2, and the prince of Greece is mentioned in Daniel 10:20.

These ruler demons are much more powerful than the worldly ones, and they have different roles to play in Satan's kingdom. Satan wants to keep us ignorant of himself, his kingdom and how it works. It's all a part of the conspiracy. If he can keep us in the dark about evil spirits and their domain, then he can also keep us defeated because we will never know who our true enemy is.

Ephesians 6:12 reads so well in the Living Bible: "For we are not fighting against people made of flesh and blood, but against persons without bodies–the evil rulers of the unseen world" (TLB). So often we are led to believe that our battle is against our wife, husband or employer, when in fact it's against demons. Perhaps initially this wasn't the case, but so often after the conflict has started in a relationship, demons are quick on the scene to exploit the situation. They often take it in a direction it would not go if it weren't for them adding fuel to the fire. There have been many occasions when my wife or I have been in bad moods or a state of depression, and there is no logical reason for it. Often it is the result of demonic oppression, and a simple authoritative prayer session can remove the depression or moodiness. For those who don't believe in the presence of demons, often their moodiness or depression progresses until the spirits have accomplished their purpose. The Bible warns us not to be ignorant of the devil's schemes, but many Christians don't take it to heart. The Apostle Paul fully knew of Satan's influence. In 2 Corinthians 2:11 he urges the people to reaffirm their love for a fallen brother and then he goes on to say: "Be of sober spirit, be on the alert. Your adversary, the devil, prowls about like a roaring lion, seeking someone to devour" (1 Peter 5:8).

Many Americans live in a Christian culture, but don't take the Scriptures seriously. They read the Bible and hear it quoted, but fail to think of it as a practical guide for daily living. They say they believe in demons and the devil, but their actions portray their disbelief.

In 1997 I was diagnosed with leukemia (I will talk more about this in Chapter 3). I had no symptoms whatsoever, but it showed up in my blood work and later, in a bone marrow biopsy. One particular Saturday night, approximately one month after I had been diagnosed, I started feeling really lousy. My body ached, and I developed a fever within a few minutes after dinner. I told my wife Debbie I was going to bed and asked her to call the associate pastors so that one of them could fill in for me the next day.

As I lay in bed, a thought came to me: Could it be possible that my symptoms were demonically induced? After all, it was eight o'clock on a Saturday night, and the week before, I had told the congregation I believed God had told me I wasn't going to die of leukemia.

Armed with that thought, I engaged the demons in some good old-fashioned spiritual warfare for about fifteen minutes. I prayed and took authority over every demon that came to my mind. I commanded the spirits of leukemia, death, sickness, and darkness in general, to leave my body in Jesus' name. To my surprise, the sickness left as fast as it came. My fever disappeared, and my body stopped aching. I ran downstairs and called out to Debbie, "I'm well! Call the guys back and tell them I'll be there tomorrow."

The scenario of my feeling ill repeated itself three more times in the next year. Each time the fever and muscle aches came, they were preceded by some significant spiritual event and, in all the cases, the symptoms left as fast as they came after a few minutes of spiritual warfare.

A similar experience occurred the Sunday night before I was scheduled to leave for Israel to host a Holy Land tour. At the conclusion of my message, I started feeling horrible. After I gave the altar call, I asked some of the men to pray for me. They did, but no one engaged in any spiritual warfare. Later, on the way home, I couldn't even sit up. I had never before felt like this. Reasoning I may be hungry, I asked Debbie to stop at Taco Bell. She did, but I couldn't eat.

On the way home, the thought occurred to me again: *Could this be another spiritual attack?*

"Let's pray," I said to Debbie. In a radical fashion, I prayed and took authority over every kind of spirit that came to my mind. Once again, within ten minutes, the sickness left. Today, most Christians I know wouldn't even *think* to engage in spiritual warfare, in such cases. It's not part of our day-to-day thinking process because we have fallen prey to Satan's conspiracy to keep us in the dark.

I must emphasize that I do not believe most sicknesses are caused by demons. What we eat, viruses, or bacterial infections—physical problems, cause most sicknesses. However, the Bible indicates there are some sicknesses caused by demon spirits.

Take, for example, the Luke 13:11-12 account: "And behold, there was a woman who for <u>eighteen years</u> had had <u>a sickness caused by a spirit</u>; and she was bent double, and could not straighten up at all. And when Jesus saw her, He called her over and said to her, 'Woman, you are freed from your sickness.'"

In today's culture, the average Christian probably wouldn't consider that demons caused such an illness. Instead of engaging in spiritual warfare, we would send her to a chiropractor. Many of us don't have a place in our theology for demons.

Many Christians become suspicious and wary when the subject of deliverances is discussed. They conclude that only "Holy Ghost whackos" would be involved in such barbaric practices. But some of the incredible demonic deliverances I've participated in have taught me a lot about God and the demonic realm.

One night, I was in Riverside, California, speaking at a regional Teen Challenge conference in the late 1990s. After I finished speaking, a few of the students hung around to ask me if I would sign their Bibles. While doing so, a couple of young women who were participants in the program approached me and asked me to pray for one of the new students they suspected might be possessed by demons. Subsequently, I introduced myself to the young lady, who was from another country, and asked her if I could pray for her. She said I could.

After a short introductory prayer, I decided to take authority over any demon spirits that were present. As I did, the young woman flew into a rage and flung herself across the tent, tearing the watch off of my arm as she went. I followed in pursuit. When I bent over her and began to pray, she tried to fight me off like a wild animal, scratching and biting at my arms. The thirty or so people in the tent looked on in bewilderment as the young girl and I wrestled on the ground. I quickly asked for their help. A number of them gathered around me and began to pray. As three of them helped me hold the girl down, she began to loudly shout out two words as she turned red in the face— "necklaces" and "strangulation." She wore no necklaces, but she acted as if she did. I took authority over the spirit of death who apparently was trying to strangle her, and then I continued. Every fifteen minutes or so, she would cry out, "Necklace! Strangulation!" Each time, after I took authority over the spirit of death and darkness, I would continue. This scenario took place throughout the two-and-a-half-hour deliverance.

At one point, I looked up at the students around us and told them they were enrolled in one of the best Christian warfare classrooms they could ever want to be in. Then I said, "Watch this! I'm going to call for some angelic help! Almost every time I do this, the demons in the person will see the angels and will respond in some way."

I prayed aloud, "Lord, please send me some angels to help! Come angels! Come angels!"

What happened next surprised even me. The voice of the spirit, spoken through the girl, cried out, "It's Michael!"

The Bible identifies Michael as an archangel (Jude 9)—an angelic warrior and the protector of Israel (see Daniel 10:13, 21; Revelation 12:7). Keep in mind that this was not an American-educated girl, nor was she a movie actress who knew the role she was supposed to play. I was used to the demon acknowledging the angels, but Michael? Give me a break! This was big-league stuff!

As the deliverance progressed, I asked the demons to reveal their names, using my best authoritative voice. I said, "In Jesus' name, I command you to tell me who you are." I repeated the command three times.

Then the voice from the girl bellowed, "Nephilim." It growled and spit as it repeated the name.

Then something surprising happened. An unfamiliar voice started an argument with the spirit called Nephilim, and said, "I told you this was a stupid idea!"

I wondered who this was and what that comment meant. So, I commanded the new demon to tell me who he was. After some hesitation he said, "My name is Anakim."

I asked one of the students to write down the names Anakim and Nephilim, because later on, I wanted to research those names in my Bible. After about two and a half hours, the young woman's countenance changed to one of peace and tranquility. Her violence subsided, and she stopped trying to bite and scratch me. She even began to smile. When she accepted Jesus Christ into her heart as her personal Savior, I knew we had won the battle.

Exhausted and amazed by what I'd witnessed, I drove back to my hotel room and got ready for bed. Before going to sleep, I checked my Bible to find out about those two characters, Nephilim and Anakim. My concordance revealed that they were both spoken of in Numbers 13:33: "There also we saw the Nephilim (the sons of Anak are part of the Nephilim); and we became like grasshoppers in our own sight, and so we were in their sight."

I thought, *They are relatives, the Nephilim and the Anakim. That's why they were together in this girl. They were inseparable!*

The girl had no way of knowing this. She wasn't educated in Scripture. What I read next really blew my mind. Written in ink in my Bible, with an arrow pointing down to the word "anak," was a notation I had written almost five years earlier, "Necklaces/strangulation." That's what Anak's name meant. This demon was a spirit who strangled people with necklaces, and in the spirit realm, this was exactly what the demon Anak was doing to this girl. He caused this girl to choke and feel as if she were being strangled with a necklace.

This girl could have easily become a candidate for a mental institution because of the conspiracy of spirits, and the slothfulness and ignorance in the body of Christ today. The Apostle Paul told us not to be ignorant of demons' schemes. But first we must believe in the reality of such creatures.

Sometimes demons can even show up at church. In Acts 16, Paul traveled to Phillipi to preach the gospel. One day, as he was going to the place of prayer, a certain slave girl, having a spirit of divination, met him and began to follow him. She kept crying out, "These men are bond-servants of the Most High God, who are proclaiming to you the way of salvation" (v. 17). The next verse tells us that she continued doing this for many days—much to Paul's annoyance. He finally turned to the girl "and *said to the spirit,* 'I command you, in the name of Jesus Christ to come out of her!' And it came out at that very moment." (Italics mine.)

Notice that the message she heralded was right on—doctrinally correct. But it wasn't *what* she said that was the problem, it was the *way* she said it. Totally out of order, she disturbed the peace. It took Paul a couple of days to catch on to the source behind the proclamation, but catch on he did. When he took authority over the spirit, he enraged a lot of people.

The devil *does* show up at church sometimes, and often he has free reign because no one is aware that he's the one behind all the chaos. We don't want to lose our sophistication and respect by suggesting that the fracas could be supported and maybe even propagated by a demonic spirit. So the spirit remains uncontested, and the church pays the price.

Let me prove my point concerning the reality of demons by sharing with you one more deliverance story. In the early 1980s, I was invited to be the special guest speaker at a youth conference at Old Oak Ranch in Sonora, California. One night, at a fireside meeting in the outside amphitheater, a young girl stood up and began to say a lot of off-the-wall stuff. And it just didn't sound right coming out of the mouth of a very beautiful seventeen-year-old girl. I looked at the pastor next to me and said, "I think this sounds demonic. Let's take her up to the chapel and pray for her."

He looked at me rather suspiciously and said, "You really think it's demonic?"

When I replied in the affirmative, about six of us took the girl up to the chapel, and what took place during the next four hours, greatly impacted all of us. It was something we would remember forever. Only later did I find out that out of fifteen pastors at this Pentecostal camp, I was the only one who really had any experience with deliverances.

I started out the session with a simple prayer for God's guidance and help. Then I slowly, but surely began to speak to the demons I believed were there. I commanded them all to tell me who they were.

They answered me in a foreign language. It sounded a lot like German. So, I commanded them to speak to me in English, and they did. I instructed them to leave the girl and, as they did, they revealed their names. One demon told me his name was "Cancer." The last demon said his name was "Lucifer." Apparently, he took on the name of Satan himself. Although demons can lie, hopefully we can force them to tell the truth. In all of the deliverances I've conducted, I haven't found too many inconsistencies in what they've told me.

The last demon, Lucifer, was a tough one—he challenged me in everything I said and did. At one point, he jeered at me and said, "Who gave you authority over me?"

I said, "Jesus did." Then, I added, "He's in this room! Jesus is in this room!"

The demon peered out through this young lady's eyes and looked around the room. Then he fired back at me, "Where is he?" And before I could answer, the spirit looked over my right shoulder and let out a blood-curdling scream. Evidently, he saw Jesus somewhere behind me. I felt more confident than usual. As the evening progressed, the demon periodically looked over my right shoulder sheepishly, and then screamed. Jesus *was* in the room!

After about an hour, he again peered over my right shoulder, but this time, instead of letting out a scream, he smiled broadly and said something I didn't want to hear. "He's gone!"

He double checked behind me, and then scanned the room with a dumb, but mean-looking, grin on his face. I said to myself, *Oh man! I'm in deep trouble now! Why did Jesus leave?* About that time, he looked directly behind the young lady and once again let out a shrill scream. Evidently, Jesus had moved to a different location in the room. Up until this time,

I didn't know God had a sense of humor. I said in a whisper, "Lord, please don't ever do that again!"

For a while, all was on track again. Lucifer's tormenting of this girl increased, and I began to tire. So I came up with what I thought was a brilliant idea. I remembered a Bible story where Jesus cast some demons into a herd of swine, after which the swine killed themselves by running off of a cliff. I recalled that there was a horse in a corral at the top of the camp. I asked someone to take over and continue praying for the girl while I asked a number of the other pastors to join me on the sidelines. I told them about my idea of casting the last demon out of her and into the horse up on the hill. I explained that I had a gun in my car, so we could shoot the horse the next morning. Surprisingly, they all agreed with me.

I went back to the girl and addressed the spirit. "I command you to come out of this girl in Jesus' name, and I'm giving you permission to go into the horse up on the hill."

The girl's eyes rolled up into her head for about fifteen seconds. Then she returned to normal. The spirit said blatantly, "There is no horse up on the hill."

I said, "You're lying. There is a horse on the hill! I'll give you one more chance to come out of this girl and go into the horse!"

Again the girl's eyes rolled up into her head for about fifteen seconds, and then she returned to normal. Once again the spirit spoke, "There is no horse up on that hill!"

I said, "Okay, have it your way! I command you to come out of this girl in Jesus' name."

Finally, after several hours, we had a complete and full deliverance. After the struggle, the young girl fell limp into our arms.

The interesting part of this story is that later that night, the Camp Director told us that for the first time in several years, they had taken that horse into the city. Apparently, the demon could exit and enter the girl at will, once he had made residence in her. By the way, I heard from her several months later, and she was doing great. She eventually married someone in the ministry.

Demons are real, and they are active in the lives of non-believers. Besides being able to occasionally cause sickness and disease, we are also told they can be instrumental in the lives of false prophets. The Apostle John wrote, "Beloved, do not believe every spirit, but test the spirits to see whether they are from God; because many false prophets have gone out into the world" (1 John 4:1).

I sometimes see preachers do some pretty phenomenal things yet they seem as fake as a three-dollar bill. Maybe they are empowered by spirits of darkness. We are told in Revelation 13:13 that the antichrist performs great signs, and that he even makes fire come down out of heaven to the earth. In verse 12 it says he's into the healing ministry also. He has a fatal wound that is healed. Not everyone who goes around healing people is necessarily from God.

In Acts 13:8-11 we are told about a man whose name was Elymas. He was known as the magician. We can assume he performed some pretty phenomenal magic, whether by the art of trickery or by a spirit's power.

Acts 8:9-11 chronicles the popularity of another magician: "Now there was a certain man named Simon, who formerly was practicing magic in the city, and astonishing the people of Samaria, claiming to be someone great; and they all, from the smallest to the greatest, were giving attention to him, saying, 'This man is what is called the Great Power of God.' And they were giving him attention because he had for a long time astonished them with his magic arts."

Before we write off Elymas and Simon as being no more than the cheap tricksters of our day–charlatans whose hands were quicker than the eye, who spent tons of money on props, mirrors and hidden cameras—we need to consider that many props available to modern-day magicians didn't exist. Even if they had, those magicians wouldn't have the money to buy them. What magicians in Bible times did, can best be described as supernatural. Remember the magicians of Pharaoh's court back in the days of Moses. These guys were really good at what they did. They did stuff that David Copperfield can only dream about. For example, they threw a stick on the ground and it became a snake. They stuck a stick in the river and the water turned to blood. By the power of their secret arts they could make frogs come out of their damp places and cover the dry land. The point I am trying to make is that there were people in the Bible who could do and say powerful things. Obviously they received their power from somewhere, but it wasn't from God. We might conclude that demon spirits can work through individuals to make them more powerful than they would be without the demon's help. When we realize this vital information, it can keep us from being deceived by "spiritual people" just because they are producing some sort of signs. The knowledge of demons and having insight into some of the ways they work can really be beneficial to our walk with God. The devil doesn't want us to be enlightened to neither the reality nor the power of his demonic realm, because he knows that his kingdom power will be weakened once it is exposed to the light. As Christians, it is our job to identify and destroy the demons' power when they get in the way of our doing God's will.

Scripture calls us to be soldiers in God's Kingdom. Every good soldier has to be knowledgeable of his enemy in order to defeat him. The Bible shows us three ways to destroy Satan and his demons' power. First of all, praise music is a very powerful tool in combating the devil's power. In 1 Samuel 16:23 it says, "So it came about whenever the evil spirit from God came to Saul, David would take the harp and play it with his hand; and Saul would be refreshed and be well, and the evil spirit would depart from him."

Over the past twenty-seven years, I have counseled many people who are being disturbed by what I believe are demonic spirits. I tell them to surround themselves with praise music, especially when they go to bed at night. I have had much success with this type of therapy. Demons don't do well in the midst of praise music. Years ago, we had a demon possessed man in our church who howled during the worship service. Often, he would have to get up during worship and go to the bathroom to splash water on his face. The spirits in him were being tormented by the praise music.

The second weapon God has given us in warring against demons is His Holy Word. Luke 4:1-13 recounts the time when the Holy Spirit led Jesus into the wilderness, where Satan himself met Him. For forty days the devil assaulted Jesus and tempted Him. Repeatedly, Jesus combated the devil's power by quoting the Word of God. "And the devil said to Him, 'If You are the Son of God, tell this stone to become bread.' And Jesus answered him, '*It is written,* man shall not live on bread alone'" (vs.3-4, italics mine.)

Jesus used the written Word against Satan three times,

each time defeating him.

There have been times in my life when I have felt uncommonly tempted, discouraged or depressed. During those times, when I've spoken Scripture aloud, I have felt relief from my trial. I don't believe it was coincidental.

The third weapon we can use against Satan and his kingdom power is what I call "direct authority and confrontation." Again, in Acts 16, a girl with a spirit of divination followed after Paul. After many days of her interfering with his ministry, he finally confronted the spirit by saying, "I command you in the name of Jesus Christ to come out of her!" (v. 18). The verse ends by stating that the demon instantly left.

This is the approach I often use in deliverances and oppressive situations in my family, as well as in prayer lines. It works. The demons are subject to our authority. I once heard a pastor use this analogy: The devil is like a thief who tiptoes around someone's house at night, trying to break in. As long as he remains unseen, he'll continue with his dastardly deed. But if the owner of the house yells, "Burglar, get out of here in Jesus' name," he'll scram. He knows he's been spotted.

Don't make the mistake of not believing in demons. But, at the same time, don't make the opposite mistake of giving them too much attention. They exist and have to be dealt with, but when you live for God with all of your heart, and pursue His divine will, often they become nothing more serious to deal with than a pesky gnat at a spring afternoon picnic. Avoid an unhealthy infatuation with demons, but do become educated about them and their ways, and learn how to deal with them properly when necessary.

# 3

# WALKING WITH GOD THROUGH CANCER

❖

*"Smooth seas do not make skillful sailors."*

—◦ AFRICAN PROVERB ◦—

*"A sickbed often teaches more than a sermon."*

—◦ THOMAS WATSON[1] ◦—

When broken, certain flowers give forth an unexpected aromatic treasure. And likewise, there can be unexpected treasures when our bodies are broken. Physical illnesses can produce brokenness—physically, spiritually and emotionally. During times of physical illness, a person often questions God's faithfulness. "Where was He when I needed Him?" "Why did He let this happen?" "Why won't He reach down and help me?"

Sincere disciples of Christ will allow these questions to lead them on a search for answers. And that search may reveal some hidden treasures. One of these treasures is humility. All of a sudden we feel like a novice in the faith again. Our self-righteous, arrogant spirit weakens as a result of our circumstances. It leads us on a new search for answers to questions we thought we would never ask.

Along with our newfound humility often comes a new dependence upon others. We find that we need real people in our lives. We're no longer able to make it by ourselves. A healthy dependence upon others to be our pillars of support and to offer counsel and encouragement enhances our lives.

One other treasure that's often discovered in the midst of physical trials is what I call a new appreciation for life. Especially during a terminal illness, each and every day seems to be a gift from God. We begin to enjoy things we used to take for granted—like a sunset, a full moon night, the sounds and smells of a warm summer night, the soothing feeling that a gentle spring breeze brings as it plays with our hair, the sound of children playing in a park nearby, the smell of a neighbor's barbecue or the warmth that's felt from a loved one's hug. It's almost as if we had let life pass by without ever having noticed these things. But sometimes God can use a physical ailment to enhance our lives in many ways.

Regarding physical illness, there are not too many things that we Americans fear more than cancer. For many, just the sound of the word brings to mind a smorgasbord of painful memories. Most of us have seen someone we love go through some sort of battle with the dreadful disease. And for way too many of us, we have also seen a lot of them lose the war.

The worst part of cancer is what it often does to a person's body before it kills them. I know of nothing more cruel and relentless than this demonic-appearing disease. It doesn't seem to be something a human being should have to endure. I hate it with all of my heart, and I believe God does too. But even for the cancer patient, there is always help when God's on the throne in their life.

I believe that if people will stay really close to God during their trial with cancer, He will guide them and deal with them in such a way that they cannot only endure it with a victorious spirit, but may even avoid its fatal conclusion. I believe that many people today would not be losing the war with a lot of terminal illnesses if they were plugged into the divine guidance of the Holy Spirit.

As you read through the following story, I hope you will pick up a new philosophy of life that will stick with you forever. Walking with God through cancer can mean the difference between life and death.

I will never forget that terrible day on January 30, 1997, when I heard the awful words: "Mr. Vietti, you have Chronic Myelogenous Leukemia."

After the doctor informed me of my diagnosis, an emergency phone call for her demanded her attention. As she left the room, she tossed a pamphlet about leukemia on my lap. There I sat, alone in the doctor's office, 150 miles from my hometown of Bakersfield, California, with no one to console me. At the last minute, my wife Debbie needed to baby-sit our granddaughter that day. Besides, it was supposed to be just a routine doctor visit for a prostate infection I thought I had.

I opened the pamphlet at random, and the very first page I turned to, read, "The person who has Chronic Myelogenous Leukemia (CML) can expect to live two to three years in a fairly normal manner by controlling the disease with medication, but at the end of this time, the Chronic Phase usually turns into an Acute Phase, and the patient succumbs to the disease." My mind spun. Two to three years of normal life left? Give me a break! That's less than the amount of time it takes to get a college degree going at a fairly rapid pace. That's less than the time of one presidential term of office. That's less time than the break between the Summer Olympics. That's no time at all. Dazed, my whole body felt numb.

*This can't be happening to me,* I thought. *It must be a bad dream that I will shortly awaken from then resume life as normal.*

No one in my family had ever had cancer—heart disease, yes, but not cancer. Through the years, I'd been careful to protect myself against heart disease. I ate my oatmeal every morning, took my daily garlic pill and stayed away from high-cholesterol foods, plus I maintained a weekly aerobic program. I was not ready to deal with cancer.

I searched my brain for reasons why this had happened to me. Maybe it was all those chemical and preservative-laden nonfat wieners I had eaten. Perhaps the electrical power lines I had lived directly under for seven years were to blame. *I should have moved when I found out about the danger of electromagnetic field force,* I thought. Wait a minute; my cancer may have resulted from the time I was crop-dusted when I was eight years old.

My cousin and I were out in the grape vineyards, in Arvin, California, watching an airplane dust the fields with chemical pesticides. We positioned ourselves right in line with the path of the plane, pretending we were American soldiers and the airplane was the enemy. As it came toward us, we raised up our invisible weapons and began to try to shoot him out of the air. It was then that the "enemy plane" dropped a load of chemical pesticides on us. I became increasingly convinced that this is what gave me cancer.

As I pondered this thought, another thought raced into my mind. The sin in my life I had tried to hide from God had given me the cancer. God was punishing me for all those secret sins tucked away in my heart. I knew, somehow, my cancer had to be my fault. I mean things like this just didn't happen without a good reason.

The doctor finally came back into the room and asked if I had any questions. I was too numb and shocked to think of any, although a myriad of questions crowded my mind later. She encouraged me to complete the other prostate tests I had come to do. I looked at her and said, "I think I just want to go home. Please cancel the rest of my tests."

As I walked into the elevator to go down to the main lobby, I felt like a dead man in the land of the living. Two women got on the elevator with me; one gave me a kindly smile and said something to me that just went in one ear and out the other. They began to talk about their plans to go to some amusement park with the kids next week, and I felt momentarily like shouting out to them, "I don't want to hear about Disneyland or Magic Mountain. What makes you think you have a right to talk about having fun while I'm dying?" I had never felt like this before. I wondered why the world didn't stop for a moment and pay tribute to a dying man. My thoughts spiraled out of control. Suddenly, I felt like I didn't belong in this world—a world designed for the living, not the dying.

As soon as I got to my car, I got a hold of myself, at least for a couple of minutes. I thought, *Ron, you're not only a Christian, but a pastor of a very large church. It's time for you to practice what you preach.*

It helps me relieve stress when I write, so I pulled out a legal tablet and wrote: "The Good Things That Can Come Out of This Illness" across the top of the page. Then I recorded my list:

I can show people how to die victoriously as a Christian;

I can share my faith in Christ with many non-Christian nurses and doctors;

I will be able to relate better and have more sympathy with others who are hurting in life;

This illness will cause me to love my family in a deeper way and appreciate them daily; and

It will cause me to live life in a fuller way than I would have, if I thought I had multiple years left on earth.

The writing helped me deal with my stress as well as refocus my attention. Then an alarming thought struck me. I needed to call home and break the news to my family. How in the world would I find enough strength to do this? Using my cellular phone, I dialed my home.

My wife answered. "Hi, Ron, how did it go?"

"Not too well," I responded. "Debbie, I have leukemia!" It was then that all the emotions I had been feeling disclosed themselves in a flood of tears.

"No Ron, that can't be!" she said, and there was silence on the other end of the phone. I could hear her breaking down in gentle, yet deep sobs.

I continued between sniffs and the breaking of my voice. "Debbie, they said I'll live for only three to four more years. I'm dying."

For the next five minutes, we sobbed over the phone. I couldn't say anymore. People in the parking lot were casually glancing over as they walked by the car. I felt sure they were thinking, "What could be that horrible?"

After a few minutes of crying, Debbie spoke between sobs. "Are you coming home?"

I told her I would as soon as I went by the motel and picked up my stuff. She wanted to know if I was going to tell the kids by phone or wait until I got home. I told her I thought it would be easier to tell them on the phone, which goes to show just how unclear my thinking was at the time. I first spoke with my son, Joshua, who was sixteen years old at the time. Joshua didn't seem to be moved by the news. He told me something I will never forget: "Dad, God has always taken care of you, and we'll just have to pray this thing away."

Later, Debbie told me that he hung up the phone, went into his bedroom and wept. My daughter, Tara, on the other hand, seemed to take it the worst. She kept repeating, "Dad, you can't die!"

I was the pastor of Valley Bible Fellowship. At the time, it was a large 2,500-member church in Bakersfield, California, and Sunday was soon approaching. How could I break this news to the congregation? I took the cowardly way out and accepted an offer from one of my closest friends Doug Loman, a former associate pastor at Valley Bible Fellowship. Doug who pastored a church in Colorado Springs, Colorado, offered—almost demanded—to fly out to Bakersfield and assist in any way he could. So I decided to let him tell the congregation. I wrote a letter for him to read, in which I explained to my church family that I didn't feel I could tell them without breaking down. With that out of the way, I needed to refocus my life and ministry, and get on with trying to live my life, for at least the time I had left.

In my twenty-five-year walk with God, I learned that there are certain people whose walk with God has developed to such a degree of maturity that they can hear God's voice and sense His will better than others. One such person is

Vicky Loman, the wife of my former associate pastor Doug Loman. She also had served on our staff for many years. Vicky was a woman who was connected to God's hotline. She and I had compared notes on many occasions when we thought God was saying something to us and, for the most part, we could usually determine what we thought God was saying. (I will say more about learning to hear God's voice in Chapter 5.) Because this was one of the rare times in my life when God seemed completely silent, I called Vicky and asked her to pray and seek God for me. She told me she would pray and call me back in a couple of days to tell me what she sensed in her heart as she prayed.

I'm a very practical sort of guy in my walk with God. I hate the idea of ever being branded as a goofy sort of Christian who hears voices all the time and lives in some mystical, out-of-touch-with-reality life. Scripture, especially the Old Testament, points to the fact that God wants a personal, interactive lifestyle with His people and, at times, He responds to people's requests in ways that are out of the ordinary. Far too many Christians today would not be able to accept a God who speaks through a burning bush, or one who instructs His people to win a war not by weapons but by marching and yelling a lot. So, although we're not to be what I would call "goofy Christians," we are to walk in a spiritual way, and that often contradicts the way we've come to see life.

After Vicky had prayed for a couple of days, she called me and told me that God had given her a peace about my illness, almost to the point that as she prayed, she couldn't help but sense a spirit of joy and victory. He also moved upon her heart to tell me to read Psalm 20:

> May the Lord answer you in the day of trouble! May the

name of the God of Jacob set you securely on high! May
send you help from the sanctuary, and support you from Zion!
May He remember all your meal offerings, and find your burnt
offering acceptable! [Selah.] May He grant you your heart's
desire, and fulfill all your counsel! We will sing for joy over
your victory, and in the name of our God we will set up our
banners. May the Lord fulfill all your petitions. Now I know
that the Lord saves His anointed; He will answer him from His
holy heaven, with the saving strength of His right hand. Some
boast in chariots, and some in horses; but we will boast in the
name of the Lord, our God. They have bowed down and fallen;
but we have risen and stood upright. Save, O Lord; may the
King answer us in the day we call.

Those were pretty good-sounding verses to me, especially the part that says, "Some boast in chariots, and some in
horses; but we will boast in the name of the Lord, our God."
God used these words in my story later on. This was the first
time since my diagnosis that a ray of hope came my way. But,
as you'll see, it was just the beginning of God's conversations
with me.

The Lord led me to a wonderful cancer doctor by the
name of Ravi Patel in Bakersfield. On my first visit, he filled
me in on all my options. He first spoke with me about the
only known possible cure for CML, and that was a bone marrow transplant. But before they could perform such a
procedure, a matching donor had to be found for me. The
best scenario for success with a bone marrow transplant is
when a sibling qualifies as a perfect match. Even though the
procedure sounded like something that belonged in the Stone
Age, I wanted to try to find a donor as fast as I could. That's

always been my nature. Let's find a solution, formulate a plan and go for it. There was about a fifty to sixty percent chance that I could have a successful bone marrow transplant providing a donor could be located. So I set the search in motion.

Dr. Patel also spoke with me about ways to possibly achieve a two-to-three-year remission, including chemotherapy, interferon and other drugs. For the time being, he told me I wouldn't have to have any treatment, but he would watch my blood count from week to week.

Dr. Patel sent me to the UCLA Medical Center to see another doctor who specialized in leukemia—Dr. Charles Sawyer. I saw Dr. Sawyer regularly as well as Dr. Patel.

My brother and sister were tested as potential donors, but neither qualified. It was then I experienced my first doubt that God would provide for me. I felt God had let me down. Surely God wanted me to be cured. He didn't want me to have to cope with the terrible stress of the unknown, did He? I knew I would have to seek Him.

Throughout the next three years, I learned what it meant to encourage myself in the Lord, as King David did in the Old Testament. As God's kids, it's important for us to see that our heavenly Father treats us much in the same manner as we do our own kids. There are occasions when He doesn't shield us from all of life's uncomfortable situations, nor does He come and bail us out right away. Instead, for various reasons, He allows us to go through some of our trials, and helps us endure them. There is no doubt in my mind that cancer has made me a better person today. So, when I heard that my brother and sister didn't qualify to be donors, I was bummed out and had to seek God for encouragement.

The following week, I received some encouraging news.

UCLA had located some unrelated donors for me. While I was ready to schedule my transplant, God had other plans. On my way back to Bakersfield from Colorado Springs, a thought came to me out of nowhere: "Ron, if you totally give yourself to God's purposes: feed the poor, evangelize the lost, and care for those in distress, then this cancer will in no way be able to touch you!"

At the same time, God gave me the Scripture found in Matthew 16:25, which says, "For whoever wishes to save his life shall lose it; but whoever loses his life for My sake shall find it."

Although this verse doesn't speak of physical life, I got the full impact of what God was trying to say, which was: "Ron, if you lay your whole life at My feet, and make Me and My will the number one priority in your life, then I will take care of you physically." Not only did I hear this thought and verse in my mind, a rush of joy and peace flooded through my body. I felt strongly that God had spoken to me, and I immediately shared it with Debbie.

For years I've taught that in order to really know if something is a word from God, there needs to be at least two to three other confirmations to the message. As soon as I got home, I went into my secret prayer chamber—my bathroom—got down on my knees and asked God to please confirm what I believed was His message. About a half hour later, I decided to go to my church office and pull something from my library that would inspire me for Sunday's message. As I combed through some of the thousand plus books that line my shelves, one book caught my attention. I pulled it off of the shelf and scanned the table of contents. One chapter looked interesting, and as I turned to it, a loose page in the book fell out. When I picked it up, there in bold print were these words: "For whoever wishes to save his life shall lose it, but whoever loses his life for My sake shall find it." Amazing! Could this be a confirmation from God?

I shared the incident with Debbie and asked, "Do you think this is God speaking to me?"

"Sure it's God," she said. Debbie my chief cheerleader told me repeatedly, "There's no way God is going to let you die. You have too much work left to do!"

The next day, I decided to share what happened with my staff to get their opinions. They concluded that God had confirmed His message to me. After being reassured by them, I went on to the next item on the staff agenda, which was to read them a short story about a WWII prisoner of war who had displayed some very godly leadership qualities. It had been months since I had last read this story. As I read the one-page article, there again, to my utter surprise, was Matthew 16:25. God seemed determined to implant that verse in my mind.

*Maybe I am going to live through this thing,* I thought. Then, another thought entered my mind. *Could He also be telling me that a bone marrow transplant would be trying to save my own life, and if I pursued that course I wouldn't make it?*

Though I believed that was the primary message God wanted to get through to me, it went even deeper, as it usually does when God speaks. The Greek word "life" that is used in the Matthew passage is *psuche,* and it can mean "ego"—the immaterial part of man no one can see. In other words, I believed God was also saying that if I continued to hold onto my ego and pride, and not give my all to Him, He would have no need to divinely intervene for me. God wouldn't kill me, because God isn't in the killing business. Of course, He can do anything He wants because He's God, and our politically right theology doesn't exclude His killing someone if that's what He wants to do. I'm merely pointing out that killing people isn't His habitual nature, which is love, mercy, kindness and grace—and for that I'm glad.

Although I needed divine intervention, God wasn't *obligated* to give that to me. Any intervention would be an act of His grace and mercy. It may not be God's will to heal every disease—a subject I'll address in Chapter 7.

What's so interesting is that in my sermon on the very Sunday before I was diagnosed with CML, I made the statement, "If you ever want God to heal you from some disease, then you better give Him a reason to keep you around."

I'm not talking about "works salvation," but I am saying that God fully expects all Christians to pray, witness, display the fruit of the spirit, and promote the Kingdom of God. We are to die to ourselves and become fully lost in His will. I believed that if I did this, God would deal with my disease.

Something important to remember is that God usually doesn't deal with any two people in the same way. What He says to me and does in my life may be totally different than what He says and does in someone else's life. The purpose of this book is not to build up the expectancy that God will act for everyone just like He did for me, but rather to encourage people to be as simple and trusting in their hearts as I was, and to fully expect God to be there like He was for me. Too many Christians complicate their lives. The Bible explicitly tells us to "be converted and become like children" (Matthew 18:3).

Hebrews 11:6 says, "And without faith it is impossible to

please Him, for he who comes to God must believe that He is, and that He is a rewarder of those who seek Him." And Proverbs 3:5-6 encourages us to "trust in the Lord with all your heart, and do not lean on your own understanding. In all your ways acknowledge Him, and He will make your paths straight."

Many Christians don't acknowledge God in *all* their ways. In the Greek, "to acknowledge," means to perceive or see. Many Christians don't even expect to see God in the midst of their trials. They don't look for Him. I believe people generally see what they are looking for, and not enough people are looking for God to show Himself in the midst of their trials. It even took me a couple of weeks before I could find God in my trial. I had to really seek Him, but when I found Him, He had a lot to say. It's a concern of mine that too many of us have not developed the spirit of approaching God like a child would approach his earthly dad in a time of need. Quite possibly it's the sin and compromise in our lives that keep us from developing this child and Abba- (Daddy)-God relationship. Somewhere along the line, we need to clean up our act, come back into the family, and become children of the living God. Little sins and compromises wreak havoc in our assurance of fellowship with God.

I just have to wonder if we make very crooked paths for ourselves by missing God in the trials of life. How many Christians among us are basically sick because they've ignored God's voice when He cried out to them, "Slow down! Your pace of life is way too hectic!" Or "Stop worrying and trust me!"

We all know that stress, if not dealt with, can really mess up our paths. I wonder how many needless divorces there are today simply because someone wasn't listening to God when He said,

"Go and apologize!" Could we be responsible for many of our own crooked paths because we're not listening for God or even acknowledging Him when He speaks to us in our trials?

On my next visit with Dr. Patel, I told him what had happened and how I believed God did not want me to go the bone marrow route. He wholeheartedly agreed with me and encouraged me to follow my heart's inclination.

Besides my doctor, a lot of loving, concerned people surrounded me. There's definitely an advantage to being a pastor of a large church when something like this happens. The people were outrageously kind and concerned for me. They sent bottles of vitamins, herbs, healing nuts and seeds. I received catalogs that contained the names of hospitals in Tijuana, Mexico. All kinds of tape cassettes, like "Dead Doctors Don't Lie," "Noni Juice Seminars," and "The Discovery of South American Healing Plants" found their way to my home. I really felt loved!

People mailed me letters and shared words they believed were from God. Some wanted me to go and be prayed for by Benny Hinn; others were convinced that if I would dip in the Jordan River seven times my leukemia would be healed. Well, I'm kind of embarrassed to admit it, but I did journey to the Jordan and dipped seven times, but to no avail. I also visited a Benny Hinn Crusade, but he didn't even call out the word "leukemia" the night I was there. I couldn't take all the different chemicals everyone sent to me. There had to be a line somewhere. All of these things couldn't be God's will for me. My mind replayed the words to an old song that said, "Everybody's talking to me, and I don't hear a word they're saying. But only the echoes of my mind!"

I knew I had to pray and tune into God's voice so I could

determine the difference between what God was really saying to me through others and what was being said just because people were wanting to make me feel better. It wasn't easy, but it was possible.

1. Thomas Watson, *Gleanings from Thomas Watson* (Morgan, PA: Soli Deo Gloria Publications, 1995). 55.

# 4

# THE HOLY SPIRIT IS THE HELPER NOT THE DOER

❖

*"And by the river on its bank, on one side and on
the other, will grow all kinds of trees for food... their
fruit will be for food and their leaves for healing."*

—∾ EZEKIEL 47:12 ∾—

This is where a lot of Christians make a fatal mistake. In John 14:16 Jesus said, "And I will ask the Father, and He will give you another *Helper* that He may be with you forever" (italics mine). And then John 15:26 says, "When the *Helper* comes, whom I will send to you from the Father, that is the Spirit of truth, who proceeds from the Father, He will bear witness of Me" (italics mine).

The Greek word for helper is *parakletos,* and it basically means "one who comes alongside to encourage, advise and speak to you."

There probably isn't a more urgent time in a person's life, than a time of terminal illness when sound counsel and advice is needed. After all, they are inundated with all kinds of information—some good and some bad. Who better to sort through everything than our creator, God Almighty? He made us, and He knows exactly what we need to do to be overcomers in our present dilemma. To help ourselves is not a sin, but to depend upon our own help to save us, is. We need to balance out our spiritual perspective with God's truth. His Word is truth.

I embarked on my own search, and began to buy a lot of books on alternative cancer treatments. I had always been somewhat of a health nut, but now I was about to go overboard, as far as some were concerned. I put myself on a radical, daily vitamin regimen, as follows:

30,000-40,000 mgs Vitamin C
25,000 IU Beta Carotene
400 IU-75,000 IU Vitamin E
50 mg B-Complex
1 g Niacin amide
400 mcg Folic Acid
50 mg Pantothenic Acid
500 mg Potassium
50 mcg Selenium
30 mg Zinc
A daily supplement of Calcium-Magnesium

I carried a backpack full of these vitamins with me everywhere I went. I later added minerals to the list and a couple of herbs. I drank only distilled water, and still do to this day. All preservatives were eliminated from my diet, and I became a vegetarian. No white bread, sugar or dairy products passed through my lips. Two glasses of green barley juice a day became part of my regimen, along with at least three pounds of carrot juice. I actually started to turn orange.

## The Holy Spirit Is the Helper Not the Doer

My diet for two years basically consisted of beans, brown rice and vegetables. And I must not forget all the green tea and Pau De Arco tea I drank daily. The health food stores loved to see me come. I probably spent approximately $300 or more a month at the health food store. Though I had no actual symptoms, my appearance resembled that of someone who was in the last stages of cancer. As I look back, I think my diet would have killed me, even if the cancer didn't.

God watched out for me though. I prayed for the Lord to lead me to a Christian nutritionist—a professional. I needed to get some balance into my life. My belief then and even now is that God doesn't want us to put a lot of garbage into our bodies. I am convinced God cares about what we eat. Why else would He have given out dietary laws to the Hebrew people in the Old Testament? Not only did I want a godly nutritionist, but also I wanted to visit an iridologist—a professional who studies people's eyes and tells them what's going on inside their body. One day my wife finally drew the line. She told me just how much she disagreed with all I was doing. What would be next, she wanted to know, a witch doctor? As I've grown in the Lord, I've come to appreciate His ways more and more. It's amazing how wonderfully He matches us up with just the right people we need in our marriages. My wife is very often God's voice to me. In retrospect, I can clearly see how I could have ruined my health and especially my immune system by almost starving myself. God used my wife to quell my radical behavior. Even in the midst of her attempts to correct me Debbie never complained about all the money I spent, and she always cooked up a pot of beans and brown rice for me. She always remembered to buy me a few gallons of distilled water. She approached me in a godly way, submitted to my desires, yet lovingly corrected me when she felt so led.

One day, I had a telephone conversation with a pastor friend who lived in Orange County. He also had a rare form of cancer. During our conversation, he casually mentioned his nutritionist. He said she was the best—a born-again Christian, who knew her stuff. He credited her with the fact that he had already outlived his primary diagnosis by several years. I asked him for her name and address, and checked out the idea with Debbie. She thought I could benefit from a nutritionist. So off we went to a place called "Ivy's Bridge to Better Health" in Tustin, California. I'll never forget the look on Debbie's face when Ivy introduced herself and then said, "Ron, would you please come over and put your head in this device? I want to look into your eyes." I winked at Debbie. Ivy was an iridologist! What a sense of humor God has. After examining my eyes, Ivy told me things about my body that medical doctors hadn't been able to explain for years. I was reminded of a verse in Luke 11:34 where Jesus said, "The lamp of your body is your eye; when your eye is clear, your whole body also is full of light; but when it is bad, your body also is full of darkness."

I wondered, could Jesus, while making a spiritual point, be using a common metaphor or a science that was widely practiced in that day? Regardless, I knew that God had led me to Ivy through my prayers. She put some balance back into my diet, and I felt good.

I still take a lot of vitamins, exclusively drink distilled water, try not to eat anything with preservatives in it, and avoid meat as much as possible except for occasional chicken and fish. I eat a lot of brown rice and beans, but have added pasta and an occasional vegetarian or tuna sandwich. I take green barley juice almost daily and occasionally drink freshly juiced carrots. I firmly believe that our bodies are capable of healing themselves of diseases, under the proper circumstances.

For example, we are told that many human bodies develop cancer cells, but an immune system and body that's operating properly deals with these cells and ostracizes them. The problem of cancer arises when our immune system stops working properly and malfunctions. We don't fully understand what causes it to malfunction, but we do know that once it stops working properly, our chief goal must be to restore it to a healthy state. Things get much more complicated when we continue to eat foods that contain a lot of pesticides and preservatives. Our bodies only have so much energy and vitality, and when they are forced to spend a large part of that energy and vitality fighting against such foreign invaders as pesticides and preservatives, they have nothing left over to fight the foreign cancer cells. They simply run out of gas, and the cancer gets worse.

It's imperative that we exchange the unhealthy food for good, nutritional food. We need food that is rich in healing properties—food that restores our liver and heart, colon, kidneys and all the rest of our internal organs, and strengthens them. For a list of these foods, consult a health food store. Usually they will have books to assist you.

Some healthy foods I'm particularly fond of are organic broccoli, spinach, cabbage, cauliflower, and other organic vegetables. If your local grocery store doesn't carry organic vegetables, ask the produce manager to special order some for you. If that's not possible, purchase some form of vegetable/fruit cleaner from a health food store. If that's not available, clean produce with simple detergent or soap and water. A nutritionist once gave an impactful visual demonstration on the importance of cleaning produce. While her family sat at the kitchen table, she pulled out a can of insect spray, sprayed freshly cut vegetables and placed the platter on the kitchen table. "Enjoy!" she said.

Like pesticides, preservatives pose a health risk. Our bodies just don't have the time or energy to put into the fighting off of these foreign invaders. Become a smart shopper. The big difference with how I eat now as compared to my diet for the first two years of my diagnosis is that now I'm not as radical. My former diet enslaved me. I was so dedicated to it that when I traveled, I would rather go a day without food than eat something inconsistent with my diet. Sometimes I would actually have my friends drop me off at a potential restaurant so I could go in and peruse the menu before deciding to eat there. Now, I realize that this couldn't have been pleasing to God. I often think back to what Jesus said when He commissioned His disciples: "And these signs will accompany those who have believed: in My name they will cast out demons, they will speak with new tongues; they will pick up serpents, and *if they drink any deadly poison, it shall not hurt them*" (Mark 16:17-18, italics mine).

I believe He was saying, in principle, that as we minister for Him, we won't have to worry about what we ingest because He will override what is bad. This is not a license to be negligent in our diet; however, this should free us.

Today, although I'm still health-food conscious, if I have to choose between having my special diet and ministering to someone over a cheeseburger at lunch, then I'll take the cheeseburger and pray for God's grace. I just want to make sure that these spiritual lunchtimes don't happen every other day.

In summary, I do the best that I can to eat healthy food, but I know that God is bigger than any nutritional regimen. Therefore I refuse to come under bondage to any diet. I must control my eating habits and not let them control me.

I'll never forget a memorable walk Debbie and I had a couple of years ago. We lived in a very beautiful place on a mini-ranch at the foot of the Sierra Mountains, which provided a beautiful backdrop for our walking prayer sessions with God. On this particular day, an idea struck me that I wanted to go to a holistic health clinic in Arizona to be injected with a bunch of vitamins and minerals. That way, the vitamins would reach deeper into my body and be more effective. When I enthusiastically shared with Debbie what God had surely dropped into my mind, I didn't get much of a response. So, I elaborated even more upon this great idea. This could be just the very thing I needed to jumpstart my broken immune system.

Instead of giving me the wholehearted support I wanted, Debbie gently said, "If you want to go to this health clinic in Arizona, then go. I don't want to stop you, but I must tell you that I don't want to go with you."

I asked her why, and she simply said, "God gave you many confirmed words and promises that you aren't going to die of this disease, and I think it would be an insult to God to keep reaching out for these 'miraculous cures.' So, go if you must, but I don't want to go. I would just discourage you if I went."

Needless to say, her lack of enthusiasm really bummed

me out. I was so ticked off that I wouldn't even pray anymore. Our walk home was in silence.

When we got home, I went into a full-fledged silent mode and pouted. Sometimes my spiritual immaturity amazes even me. Debbie came into the living room and sat down on the couch. "Ron," she said, "if it's really bothering you that much, then why don't we talk to God about it. Let's ask Him to give us a word, and then we can rest in what He says to us."

This is the way Debbie and I live out our lives with God. It's so simple and childlike, that many people criticize us as being too simplistic. Yet we view this manner of life as being the way God, through Scripture, has instructed us to live.

I opened our prayer time and said, "Lord, you know I am really bummed out. For some reason You have not chosen to heal me yet, and I am getting a little impatient. Please forgive me for my attitude. I believe I've really come up with a good idea in going to this clinic in Arizona, but Debbie doesn't think it's a good idea. So, right now, we ask you to either confirm this idea with a word, or give us a word that would show us that this is not Your will. In Jesus' name we pray, amen."

We waited in silence for a few minutes. After about five minutes I asked Debbie, "Did God put any verse or thought in your mind?"

"Well, I don't know if it was God or not, but I got James 1:7."

"Okay," I said. "Get the Bible and read what it says."

She picked up a modern translation and read, "When a man hears God speak to Him, he shouldn't be double-minded, for double-minded people receive nothing from God."

Both Debbie and I believed we knew what that meant. God had told me in many ways that He was going to take care of me, but I was becoming double-minded. Though, at the time, we both thought that's what His message was, neither of us voiced our opinion.

Debbie asked, "Did God give you a verse?"

And I replied, "Yes He did, but I'm not familiar with the passage. It's Isaiah 31:1."

I reached for my Bible, opened it to Isaiah, and read the verse. I couldn't believe my eyes. It said, "Woe to those who go down to Egypt for help, and rely on horses, and trust in chariots because they are many, and in horsemen because they are very strong, but they do not look to the Holy One of Israel, nor seek the Lord!"

With a silly little grin on her face, the kind that really rubs in the fact that she's right and I'm wrong, Debbie asked, "Do you still want to go to Arizona?"

"No," I confessed. "I really didn't want to go a lot anyway. I was just testing you to see how spiritual you were."

"Right," she said.

God knew vitamins would not be the source of my healing—only He would be. He has never convicted me for taking vitamins, because I still do today. I believe, however, that He wanted me to understand that there was a line of balance that I had to maintain in my life, and that He and His words to me had to remain my number one hope for healing.

# 5

# LEARNING TO
# HEAR GOD'S VOICE
❖

*"To go as I am led, to go when I'm led, to go where
I am led, it is that which has been for twenty years
the one prayer of my life."*

—∽ A.T. PIERSON [1] ∽—

*"Belief that divine guidance is real rests upon two
foundational facts: first, the reality of God's plan for
us; second, the ability of God to communicate with
us; on both of these facts the Bible has much to say."*

—∽ J.I. PACKER [2] ∽—

I had been diagnosed for almost six months, and my white
blood cell count continually went up and down. Dr. Patel
tried to control it with a drug called "hydrea." I still remember
those dreaded biweekly trips to the doctor's office to undergo
blood tests. I prayed all the way to the doctor's office, "Oh
God, I need a good blood test. Please help my blood to be
healthy, and my white blood cell count to be low . . ."

I usually brought my Bible with me, so I could work on
my weekly Bible study while I waited. Eventually, the hospital staff would call me back and poke me in the arm with a
needle. They'd take a couple test tubes of blood out, and then
I would wait in the lobby for the results. I still remember the
stress of waiting and praying.

Every time the nurse would come to the door to call for a patient, my heartbeat would race, thinking they were bringing me my blood test report. Would my white blood cell count be good or bad, high or low? I waited nervously. The normal range for a white blood cell count is between 4,000-11,000. For months my white count would be high, sometimes anywhere from 15,000 to 65,000. And then when I would raise the dosage of my medicine, it would slowly go back into the normal range again.

In accordance with my blood test, the doctor regulated my intake of medicine. The drug hydrea could control my leukemia for a couple of years. Eventually, it would lose its effectiveness over time. "When?" was the question that grated on my mind. I also made regular trips down to UCLA to see Dr. Charles Sawyer. After months of being on hydrea, he approached me with the idea of trying a clinical study that combined two potent drugs: alpha interferon, an immune system building drug, and chemotherapy. I decided to participate in the trial, hoping the treatment would produce a temporary remission in my body. Several times a day, either my wife or I would inject these drugs into my body. The side effects of the alpha interferon consisted of flu-like symptoms. I would develop a fever of about 101-102 degrees in the middle of the night. It would last about an hour and a half, then I would perspire so profusely that I would have to change my clothes before going back to sleep. The idea was to trigger my immune system to kick in and fight it off. Every night before I went to bed, I would place some aspirin and water nearby so I could reach over and take some about two hours before I had to get up. Without the aspirin, I couldn't get out of bed because my body ached so badly, and once up, it wasn't long before I had to inject myself with a dose of chemotherapy. Then I would get sick all over again.

My appetite and taste for food took a nosedive. I would sit in restaurants and just stare at my food. This was no way to live. I couldn't concentrate, and I had difficulty preaching. Weeks went by, and not only did I not get better, I started getting huge dime-sized canker sores in my mouth and a terrible case of hemorrhoids. My body didn't tolerate the drugs, and the Lord only knows how badly the ministry suffered because of this.

I'll never forget one Saturday night late in 1997. While Debbie and I lay in bed, I said, "This can't be God's will for my life. These drugs are tearing me up! Let's ask God for a sign to determine if it's His will for me to continue with these drugs." So, I prayed this simple prayer: "God, if it's Your will for me to get off these drugs, then please cause Belinda to come up to me at church tomorrow and give me a divine word. If You do, I'll know that's a sign from You that I'm not to be on these drugs any longer."

Debbie added, "Lord, don't only send Belinda up with a word for Ron, but also cause Charlie Garcia to have a special word for him also. Amen!"

Very seldom do people spontaneously give me special words on Sundays. I did receive many words of encouragement the first few weeks after my diagnosis, some of them prophetic. However, for the most part, they had all pretty much ceased by this point.

After Debbie and I prayed, I thought, *Fat chance of both Belinda* and *Charlie coming up to me on Sunday morning and giving me a word from God!*

Isn't it odd how fickle our faith is when we pray? We ask God to do mighty and wonderful things. Sometimes we even end our prayers with little catchy phrases like: "And I know you'll do this for your glory. Amen." Then, we mutter under our breath, "Fat chance He'll do this, but oh well I prayed it anyway!"

All I can say is I'm so glad that the answers to my prayers don't always depend upon my faith. I knew God *could* do this, but I guess deep down in my heart I just really didn't know *if* He would.

On Sunday morning, in between the first and second service, Belinda came up to me and said, "Pastor Ron, I have a word for you."

*Wow!* I thought, *This has to be really good.*

She said, "I had a vision, and I saw you out in the middle of a lake in a boat without any oars. I felt really sorry for you and wanted to swim out to help you, but God said, 'Don't go! This is exactly where I want Him for now!'"

Well, that certainly was one-half of the answer to our prayers. Although I didn't really like what she said, I knew in my heart that God had spoken. There were some things He wanted to do in my life before He healed me. I accepted the word, but remembered only half of our prayers had been answered.

Charlie attended the third service that day, and he sat right in the front row. After the service was over, he got up and went home. So I thought Belinda's word—although right on—was just a fluke, a coincidence.

After the service, I gathered together my stuff, had a few short conversations, and headed for the parking lot. Before I could get into my car, I saw Charlie Garcia walk across the front lawn toward me.

"Ron," he said, "I went home, and God told me to come back to the church and give you a word."

I thought, *This is just too good to be true. God is really answering Debbie's and my prayers.*

Charlie said, "God gave me Zechariah 4:6: 'Not by might nor by power, but My Spirit says the Lord of hosts.' Does that mean anything to you?"

"Does it ever!" I replied.

I went home, anxious to tell Debbie the news. On the way, I looked in the back of my Hebrew-Greek key study Bible for the Hebrew meaning of the words "might" and "power." The Hebrew word for "might" is *chayil* and is a derivative of another Hebrew word, *chuwl,* meaning, "to cause to tremble, to twist, to shake, to writhe with pain." Immediately I thought of the alpha interferon. That drug caused me to tremble with night chills and to twist a lot with fever and sweats. I couldn't even get up in the morning because my body was racked with pain.

Then I looked up the Hebrew word for "power." The word was *kowach,* meaning, "potency—strong substance." I related this to the chemo drug. It was so laced with power, potency and strength that if I accidentally dropped it on my skin it would burn.

I had my two words from God. He basically told me that no drug would save me, at this point, and that it was useless to continue taking them.

I wondered how many people took drugs without consulting God first. Our heavenly Father has an opinion about most of the things that concern us, but we don't bother to consult Him very often. I shudder to think about what might have happened to my body had I continued to take these powerful drugs. It quite possibly could have meant a death sentence for me. However, in some people's cases, it might mean a death sentence for them if they *don't* take chemotherapy. I'm quite sure that it is God's will for some people to be on these powerful drugs. Please don't ever assume that what God says to one person, He automatically means for everyone. The point is, we must all learn to hear God for ourselves. It's crucial that we learn to tap into His voice and develop a good listening ear. If I've learned any one valuable thing in my almost thirty years of walking with God, it's that He likes to talk to His people. The Lord said to the Church of Laodicea: "Behold, I stand at the door and knock; if anyone hears My voice and opens the door, I will come into him, and will dine with him, and he with Me" (Revelation 3:20).

The word "dine" creates a word picture for us; one that God wanted us to see. It's a picture of a family kicking back at the dinner table after a hard day's work. As they sit around the table, they visit with one another.

"How was your day, Son?"

"Good, Dad! Could you please pass me the corn?"

"Did you have any problems today at school?"

"As a matter of fact, I did, and I was meaning to ask you for some advice, Dad."

That's the idea in Revelation chapter three. God wants intimacy with us. He always has and always will. Throughout the pages of Scripture from the Old to the New Testament, God has demonstrated His desire to communicate and interact with His people. He wants a personal relationship with His kids—just like an earthly dad would want with his children.

Have you ever wondered why God used the word "father" to describe his relationship with us instead of another word like "taskmaster," "chief," "boss in heaven," "employer," or even the word "Your Superior"? He chose the word "Father," so we would perceive Him correctly.

Abraham saw the Son of God and conversed with Him on at least several recorded occasions. It might have been a lot more common occurrence than we think. God spoke to and had a personal interaction with Jacob. The same can be said of Noah, Gideon, Elijah, Elisha, Isaiah, Jeremiah, Daniel, Ezekiel, Hezekiah, and others. Among those in the New Testament Jesus spoke with were Peter, John, Paul and Cornelius.

There is absolutely nothing in the Bible that even hints that God has ceased speaking to His people today. God speaks by many different means. When I say "God speaks," I mean He communicates an idea. It doesn't mean He audibly talks to us. He can speak to us through dreams, visions, prophetic words, sermons, circumstances, other people, Scripture, cassette tapes, books—even through Christian television.

If God speaks to His people, our job is to learn how to hear. Jesus said, speaking of a shepherd, "When he puts forth all his own, he goes before them, and the sheep follow *him because they know his voice*" (John 10:4, italics mine). I cannot stress enough the importance of learning to hear our Shepherd's voice. As I said in an earlier chapter, knowing how to hear God's voice can have a tremendous impact on our lives. In fact, if I had not learned to hear His voice and sense His Spirit's guidance early in my Christian walk, who knows where I would be today. I wouldn't be in the ministry nor would I have written this book. I definitely wouldn't be married, and I would probably be dead. That's how important it was for me to develop a *personal* relationship with God. His voice has been a lamp for my feet.

"My sheep hear My voice, and I know them, and they follow Me" (John 10:27). Scripture indicates that those who were really in tune with God heard His voice in one way or another.

One of the saddest things in Christendom today is the unwillingness of God's people to listen when God speaks. It takes time and discipline in the believer's life to become sensitive to the Holy Spirit. And there's a price we will pay if we don't learn to hear!

Probably six months before I was diagnosed with leukemia, I heard a voice in my inner man speak to me about changing my diet and dealing with the stress in my life. And the voice spoke to me repeatedly. Every time I picked up a book on the subject or watched a television infomercial that dealt with health and diet, conviction settled in, yet I did nothing about it. In hindsight, I believe God was trying to tell me to eat better and live better, but I didn't listen. It's so simple to learn to hear God's voice and walk with Him in a personal relationship. Yet many people fail to enter into a conversational relationship because they have somehow perceived it to be difficult to live this way.

Jesus said, "My yoke is easy, and My burden is light" (Matthew 11:30). It's really not difficult to walk with the Lord in a pleasing way.

The Lord drove home this point to me in a very simple way. One day, I thought about how at marriage seminars we teach Christian dads to be more affirming to their kids. As I pondered over what we teach our earthly fathers to do, it dawned on me that if that's what we expect out of good earthly dads, could we expect the same out of God? I think the answer is yes. However, if that's the case, then why doesn't the average Christian hear God affirm him more? When was the last time you heard God say something affirmative to you? When was the last time God spoke to you and said, "Good job!" or "I'm proud of you!" or "I appreciate you!" If His yoke is really easy and His burden is light, then I would suppose that more often than not we hit the mark in our service to Him.

It's easy to serve God. If, for example God brought a person to your mind, and you pray for that person, then you've just served God one time that day. If later that same day you feel led to call someone and leave a Scripture verse on their answering machine, you've just served God twice that day. Then, in the evening, if you go over to someone's house with a cake you've baked, and mention that God loves him or her, then you've just served God for the third time that day. Satan has lied to us saying it's hard to serve God. Then he discourages us from even trying. God's yoke is easy, and the burden He asks us to carry is light.

Sometimes I feel sorry for God. I'm sure there are occasions when He looks down upon this earth and sees maybe a lonely widow with no one caring for her needs. He probably hurts for her and thinks, *If I only had a body, I would go to her house to sit and talk with her.* Maybe He sees a young person who uses a wheelchair, who has no teenage friends. The teen sits there every Friday and Saturday night at home, while all the other teenagers in the community go out to church concerts, take in a movie and then go to the ice cream parlor. God looks down on this teenager and thinks, *If I only had a young body, I would call together other kids in the church, and we would all go over, pick her up, and take her with us to the concert, the movies, and then to the ice cream parlor.* Perhaps God thinks, *If I had a body, I would travel to the foreign mission field on my vacation and help the poor. With the use of a body, I would call people on the phone and encourage them in the Lord. I would get a job, make a lot of money and give it to the church and to the poor.*

I'm here to tell you, God *does* have a body, and that body is us. Our bodies belong to Him. We are the only body He has. The only mouths, ears, eyes, arms and hands He has, and we need to do what Paul in Romans 12:1 says to do: "I urge you therefore, brethren, by the mercies of God, to present your bodies a living and holy sacrifice acceptable to God, which is your spiritual service of worship."

Here's the point I'm driving at: Jesus is the head of the body, and He lives in heaven while we, His body, are still here on the earth. As the body of Christ, we must be sensitive to the head's direction. The head does the thinking and makes the decisions for the body based upon His infinite wisdom and sovereign outlook. Our job is to simply obey. Just as our body parts don't do their own thing without the mind instructing them, we shouldn't do our own thing without God's direction, guidance and His word. Again, we are to trust in the Lord with all of our heart and lean not on our own understanding. He is the head and the brains of this whole kingdom of life we live. Sometimes, He will ask us to do things we will never understand until we get to Heaven. But by faith, we must obey Him and leave the reasoning up to Him.

There are several ways we can hear God's voice. One of the ways is what I call the "Culmination of Facts Method." In Acts 16:6 it says, "And they passed through the Phrygian and Galatian region, having been forbidden by the Holy Spirit to speak the word in Asia." Now we don't know what the Holy Spirit did to forbid them to preach in that area, but He did something they must have recognized as being from God. The very next verse says, "And when they had come to Mysia, they were trying to go into Bithynia, and the Spirit of Jesus did not permit them."

Here we have the Apostle Paul and his fellow servants trying to preach the word in various regions, and the Spirit of God did not allow them to go. In verse nine it says that Paul had a vision of a man in Macedonia who appealed to Paul to come over there and help them. Paul concluded that God wanted him to go to Macedonia. Paul simply put together two plus two plus two and came up with six.

Sometimes God does one thing here and something else over there, and then He causes one more thing to happen. All three events agree and lead us to the same conclusion that God is speaking. To give a more personal example let me use my leukemia again. God said something to me through Belinda, then through Charlie, using Scripture. On top of those two things, He deeply convicted me through prayer that I was to be through with the drugs I was taking. He also gave Debbie and I some radical verses that said I was not to trust in these medicines to save me. If all four of these things lined up and pointed toward the same message, then I could conclude God was speaking to me. That's the essence of the "Culmination of Facts Method"—three or four different things happening that carry a unified, strong message.

Another way a Christian can hear God is through other people. One time I tore a rotator cuff in my shoulder. The doctor ordered x-rays and examined my shoulder. He advised me to undergo shoulder surgery as soon as possible and said he wanted to order an MRI. When he left the office to make the arrangements for the MRI, I prayed for God to either confirm the direction of the doctor or guide me in another.

Jesus said we should pray at all times and never lose heart (ref. Luke 18:1). The Apostle Paul said to "pray without ceasing" (1 Thessalonians 5:17). Throughout the day, we should be in a conversation mode with God. If we didn't have recurring needs popping their heads up all day, then why would Paul tell us to pray all the time? Paul wrote, "But he who is spiritual appraises all things, yet he himself is appraised by no man. For who has known the mind of the Lord, that he should instruct Him? But we have the mind of Christ" (1 Corinthians 2:15-16).

So, while the doctor lined up an MRI for me, I prayed. When he came back, I already had a check in my spirit about the MRI. I said, "I don't know how I feel about having an MRI because I have been diagnosed with leukemia. Through my study of the disease and its causes, I've come to see that electromagnetic fields can possibly cause and enhance leukemia in people, so I'm not so sure an MRI would be good for me. So, if you don't mind I would like to pray about it for a couple of days."

The doctor said that he understood my concerns, but didn't think an MRI would be bad for me. This all took place about two o'clock on a Wednesday. I went directly home and prayed on the way home for God to give me guidance. That night our church had its regular Bible study with about fifteen hundred people in attendance. As soon as the Bible study was over, an elderly lady named Tasha, who is really connected to God, came up to me and said, "Pastor Ron, I have something God wants me to tell you. I don't know how to explain it any better than this: I saw you get into a tanning bed, and God told me to tell you not to go into tanning beds because they are not good for you."

As I look back, I can't believe that I didn't get it right away. I must have really been tired after the Bible study. All I could think of was, *I don't go into tanning beds.*

Now, I must remind you that in our church people don't always come up and randomly give out words to me. I would say that this kind of thing happens maybe eight or ten times a year. When I went home that night and lay in my bed, I reflected on what Tasha said, and I prayed, "Lord, if this was from you then please reveal the meaning to me."

No sooner did I get those words out of my mouth than I got the answer. The tanning bed described the MRI equipment. God had specifically answered my prayer and told me to not have an MRI, just short of six hours after I had prayed about it.

Another important way a person can hear God is through the written Word (the Holy Scripture). Hebrews 4:12 says, "For the Word of God is living and active and sharper than any two-edged sword, and piercing as far as the division of soul and spirit, of both joints and marrow, and able to judge the thoughts and intentions of the heart."

The whole idea and message of God's gospel is called the *logos* of God, in Greek. However, when God decides to take part of that whole message and personalize it to us, then it's called *rhema.* God takes part of His Word and puts our name on it.

Most of us experience God's voice this way when the pastor gives his sermon, and the Scripture he uses seems to speak directly to us. We feel like God's chosen that particular text with us in mind. So often after a service people will approach me and tell me that that particular sermon was just for them. They felt like they were the only person in the building. That's the way *rhemas* often work.

At other times, we sense God speaking to us as we read His Word in our devotion time. One verse might hop right off of the written page and hit us right between the eyes. Usually that's God speaking to our hearts. This kind of communication from God to our hearts must be pretty common, whether we acknowledge it all as coming from Him or not. Jesus said, "It is written, 'Man shall not live on bread alone, but on every word that proceeds out of the mouth of God'" (Matthew 4:4). The Greek word for "word" here is *rhema*—a word with your name on it. In other words, according to Jesus, we need to hear the spoken Word of God in our hearts as much as we need food to live.

Once, when I was battling the blues because of some bad blood reports, I received a message from a man named Paul. He had attended our church almost eighteen years earlier, but had moved away to Washington. He had visited the church in mid-March, while I was away speaking in Colorado. He left a message for me stating that he had also been diagnosed with CML three years earlier. He wanted me to know that he felt he was being healed. He had been in remission for longer than two years and felt great. He told a member on my staff to tell me that this disease wasn't as bad as some people made it out to be. It could be beaten.

That bit of encouragement really brought my spirits up, and they stayed up for quite a while. About two months later, after struggling through a particularly tough day, I decided to call Paul in Washington to see how he was doing. He encouraged me so much with his message the first time, I needed to call him again for some more of that encouragement. But this time it wasn't to be. I discovered that Paul was the one who needed encouragement. He had just found out that his leukemia had come out of remission; his blood cell counts skyrocketed. I ministered to him the best way I could—gave him some Scriptures and prayed for him.

I felt really bad for the guy. He had no wife to encourage him, like I did and, as far as I knew, he had no kids nearby. When I got off the phone, the blues set in. I sat in the living room, stared at the walls and tried to sort it all out. I didn't sit there very long before I received a telephone fax from one of the women in our church. It was a poem. The middle of the poem quoted Habakkuk 2:3. "For the vision is yet for the appointed time; it hastens toward the goal, and it will not fail. Though it tarries, wait for it. For it will certainly come, it will not delay."

Those were some good verses. I sent up a quick "Thank-you Lord for those words!"

The Bible says two or three witnesses can confirm every fact (ref. Matthew 18:16). I rarely accept a single verse or a prophetic word by itself, unless it is very detailed and exact. I do use simple verses divinely given to me, as confirmations to other things, but when possible I like confirmations to messages like these. Could this poem be a coincidence, or was it really a divine word from God?

I didn't have to wait too long to find out. Two days later, I went to my office to do some work. I hadn't been there for about a week. I pulled out a notebook from my desk to record some notes. Out fell a piece of paper, which read: "Habakkuk 2:3."

I was elated! It seemed as though God went out of His way to get a message to me. And stuff like this happened many times. I would become discouraged, and God would pick me up. What a yo-yo type of existence! Regularly, I had to do what King David did—encourage myself. So often, there is no one else to encourage us, so we must learn to encourage ourselves.

God often speaks to me through what I call "the inner ear method." For years, I wondered what Jesus meant when He said, "He who has ears to hear, let him hear" (Matthew 11:15). Usually, when Jesus used this phrase, it was right after He had said something in a story or parable. What He meant was, we can see beyond the physical realm and hear more than what our physical ears hear. In other words, we must develop our spiritual senses so we can understand more than the obvious. The Spirit of God has the ability to take us behind the scenes of any circumstance and teach us lessons that the unredeemed couldn't learn even if they wanted to.

Sometimes God takes the ordinary, common objects and reveals a deeper meaning— something we would not normally perceive. The Bible tells us that we have ears in our heart with which to hear. It's hard to comprehend that God has given us Christians so many spiritual gifts, and we don't even bother to use them. I mean, God went out of His way to bless us with everything we need, and more–so we can live a successful Christian life. In fact, Peter put it this way: "… His divine power has granted to us everything pertaining to life and godliness" (2 Peter 3:1a).

We have it all, folks!

This is how spiritual ears work. Jerry Cook, a pastor in Washington, put it this way many years ago: "Have you ever had a strong hunch that something is true or ought to be a certain way? And the hunch just stays there day and night? Well, friend when you get saved, your 'huncher' gets saved too!"

God can, at any time, speak to us through any of the methods I've mentioned. He can also use spiritual dreams and visions. I haven't had more than five or six of these occurrences in my life, but each one was very valuable to me.

With my leukemia keeping me in an up and down state, I had to battle against discouragement regularly. Demonic doubts crept into my heart that told me that I was going to die, especially every time I had a bad blood count on my tests. Sometimes I even found myself planning my own funeral. I went as far as to write both of my children letters, have Debbie seal them and put them away, so if I died I could have one last chance to share what was on my heart.

But here's the miraculous part of my story I want to relate. Every time I became discouraged, God sent a "word" to me to bring me up again. He used all sorts of methods, but the result was always the same. In my depression, I'd cry out to Him for a word of encouragement—affirmation that He was still there. And He never failed me, not even once. But again, I was the type of person who *expected* to see Him, when I called out to Him.

Let me show you what I mean. I was invited to speak at a men's conference up in Sacramento a few years ago. After the service, the pastor asked the men to lay hands on me and pray for me. And as they gathered around me, two or three of them led the others in prayer. The second man who prayed really spoke to my heart. "Lord," he began, "every time Ron tends to get down, supernaturally give him some encouragement to bring his spirits back up and put some faith back into his heart."

Not only was God already doing that, but it was something I needed Him to continue doing.

A few weeks later, that prayer was answered again. My blood tests were headed back into the normal ranges, and I was elated. I was so optimistic that God was going to heal me, that every time I got a good blood test, I would think *He's healing me! This is really it this time!* But usually the results didn't remain good.

This time, however, my blood tests had been good for three weeks. Just when everything was going well, I came down with the flu and felt lousy for quite a while. *Oh boy,* I thought, *just what I need when I start doing well.*

I had a scheduled blood test during this time, and the results were awful. My white blood cell count was nearly 32,000—almost three to four times as high as it should be. Discouragement and anger made my spirits take a dive.

As soon as I was home from the doctor that day, I marched straight into my prayer closet and began to encourage myself in the Lord. I prayed, "Lord, I'm going down again. But that's okay because I believe You told me through a brother's prayer in Sacramento that every time I got down you would send a word or sign of encouragement to strengthen my faith. So God, it's time for You to do that. I have a need today. Thank You for I know You won't let me down."

As I walked out of my prayer closet, I glanced at the phone and said aloud, "God, You're going to have someone call me. I know You are, so I'm going to sit here and wait for that encouragement." I plopped down by the phone and waited.

The Bible says that "faith is the assurance of things hoped for, the conviction of things not seen" (Hebrews 11:1). When the phone rang I yelled, "I knew it!"

This was going to be good! "Hello," I said, fully expecting a word from God. But it was only my daughter wanting to talk to my wife. Undaunted, I didn't budge. I had faith in my heart that God had put there. So, I waited another five minutes, and the phone rang again. My heart raced. What did God want to say to me?

"Hello," I said. But this time it was my son just shooting the breeze. But that was okay. I had heard God speak before, and He wasn't about to let me down now. I resolved to sit there all night, if necessary, until God spoke to me.

I stared at the phone. A few minutes went by, and it rang again. This time it was Belinda Mattly, the woman who had given me very valuable words a couple of times before. "Ron, I can't get you off my heart," she said. "I felt like God wanted me to call you today and tell you not to be discouraged and *don't pay attention to blood tests.* Keep your eyes on Him, and He'll come through for you!"

He did exactly what I expected Him to do. My spirit soared. Every time I became downcast, God was there to lift me up. He talked to me all along the way. Ever since the day of my diagnosis, He has conversed with me. He has guided me. But the best was yet to come.

1. Arthur T. Pierson, *The Gospel, Vol. 2* (Grand Rapids, MI: Baker Book House, 1978), 8.

2. J.I. Packer, *Knowing God* (Downers Grove, IL: InterVarsity, 1973), 210.

# 6

# FINDING GOD'S PROMISE TO YOU

❖

*"We have twenty five cents—*
*and all the promises of God."*

—⌁ HUDSON TAYLOR ⌁—

*"I have thumbed my Bible many a year: I have never*
*yet thumbed a broken promise. The promises have*
*all been kept to me: Not one good thing has failed."*

—⌁ CHARLES H. SPURGEON ⌁—

M y confidence level soared. I wasn't going to die from this dreaded disease, or at least that's what I believed. In fact, I was so elated about all the fantastic signs God had shown and confirmed to me that I began to include many of these stories in my sermons on Sunday. Those sermons traveled the radio waves to several different states. Most everyone in the church, as well as those in our national radio audience, believed with me that I wouldn't die. Although I had convinced everyone else that I would live, my body wouldn't comply. It wouldn't submit itself to the way I thought things were supposed to be. My blood count remained unstable. I had to maintain a continual dose of self-encouragement. For the most part, God encouraged me Himself. I began to notice that when I abided in the Holy Spirit, my optimism rose, but when I stopped abiding in His Word and fellowship, and began to feast my mind more on medical books and what they had to say about my disease, discouragement prevailed. There was a marked difference in my emotional state and confidence level when I walked in the Spirit as opposed to when I distanced myself from Christian fellowship, God's Word and prayer. I needed to stay in the Spirit all the time. I had my share of discouragement, but hopefully it never showed. Usually, I could get myself back up after spending an hour with the Lord. Remarkably, God's grace *was* sufficient for my need.

People often commended me on how strong I was and how brave I was to be able to face such an awful diagnosis with such optimism. I was always quick to tell them that all the glory belonged to God because it was He who gave me the strength to get through it.

In fact, a thought hit me one day in my devotional time with God, that we Christians probably give too much credit to people in the Bible like David, Daniel and Shadrach, Meshach and Abednego—the three Hebrew youths taken captive with Daniel—for their great victories in the faith. We admire David for having the courage to take on Goliath. We are impressed with Daniel as he faced the lions with his hope fixed strongly on God. And oddly enough, Daniel's friends weren't afraid of the fire. After walking through my leukemia with God, I have to wonder if we're not sometime guilty of giving the glory to the wrong person. If any one of us truly abided in God as David did daily, we could fight and be victorious over our Goliaths too. And if we all prayed three times a day to God like Daniel did, we could bravely face the lions in our lives, as well as courageously join Shadrach, Meshach and Abednego in the fire. When we do conquer our

Goliaths, face our lions or fiery trials, perhaps we give the glory and the praise to the wrong people. It is God who gives us the strength to brave life's stormy seas. For me, I knew it was God because I saw the contrast firsthand of how weak I was without Him and how strong I became with Him. Psalm 18:32 tells us that it's God who girds us with strength.

One day I wasn't girded up in the Spirit like I should have been. I had received one of the worst blood tests ever. Distraught, I began to weep on the way home. I finally pulled my car over to the side of the road and prayed: "Lord, I'm not afraid to die; You know that. But God what hurts me is that I've told all these people that You're not going to let me die. But my body keeps on doing badly! Oh God, all these people need is to hear another flaky Christian tell them that he has heard God tell him he's not going to die, and then keel over on them. That's going to injure their faith in You, and make me look like a real nut case, and God I don't want to go down that way. You've given me a lot of signs up until now, but for the most part, they've all come through other people! God, I beg you to give me personally a promise from You that I can lean on throughout the remainder of this trial. Now, I know that You're not obligated, and I won't ask You again anymore after this. In Jesus' name, amen."

After I prayed, excitement welled up inside me that He was really going to do it. I did something that day in my car that I would never encourage anyone else to do, unless God specifically instructed him or her. I asked God to send an angel to my car and cause me to spontaneously open up my Bible to a passage that God wanted me to read. Whatever it was, I promised I would never ever doubt it for the rest of my life. If I was going to die, then I wanted to know. If not, I wanted to know that. I called on the angel to come and be God's messenger, and I waited a couple of minutes to give him time to get there. Then I simply said, "In Jesus name," as I opened my Bible and pointed to a random passage. Before I even looked, I took time to thank God for this promise He had given me. There was no doubt that this was from God. The verse my finger rested on was Psalm 91:7: "A thousand may fall at your side, and ten thousand at your right hand; but it shall not approach you. You will only look on it with your eyes." I praised God and shouted out some words of praise! Surely this was from God. I mean, how in the world could I get any better or plainer verse than this? God knew me so well.

I'm the kind of person who doesn't expect special privileges. When a parishioner takes me to lunch, I don't expect him to pay for it simply because I'm his pastor. Nor do I ever expect a free haircut from a parishioner or a special price on a car. In the same way, if I saw someone else suffer and die from cancer, in the back recesses of my mind I would think that I should likewise die. Knowing that, God told me not to base the outcome of my trial upon what happened to other people. He also told me very plainly that this disease would not come upon me; that I would only look upon it with my eyes. That's exactly what was happening. I had never yet had any symptoms of the disease, but I could look upon its presence with my eyes when I looked at my blood reports. I knew this promise had to be from God, even though I got the word in a not-so-practical way.

I know that some people may scoff and ridicule me for the way I got this word, but more than likely, these same people would respond to Abraham the same way if they had lived in his day, when he said he'd heard God tell him to pack up and leave Haran. They probably wouldn't be able to contend with Joshua's apparent instructions from God as to the way to wage war with the people of Jericho. And most assuredly, they would have probably wanted Moses committed to a mental health institution for saying that God appeared to him in a burning bush! The Apostle Paul's conversion testimony would also be held in contempt. Yes, I received my promise from God in a non-conventional way, but I'll take it anyway it comes. I knew God had spoken to me. But it was just the beginning of Him speaking to me directly.

Almost a month later, during a sermon, I scolded some of the people in the congregation for bellyaching about not being able to be involved in a ministry because of work schedules or because they were shut-ins or because they felt trapped at home with little babies. They complained that they didn't feel good about themselves, and wanted me to find a ministry for them. I told them to stop complaining, go home and get out their phonebooks, and pray for spiritual guidance as they chose names of people they could write to, telling them about Jesus. I maintained that God could make this a form of ministry for them, and that He could use it to touch people's lives. They could start telling people they had a "phonebook gift."

The next day, I drove my wife to the bank, and as I sat in the parking lot contemplating my sermon I thought, *Hey, maybe I should try the phonebook thing.* The thought entered my mind repeatedly. Finally, it dawned on me that this wasn't just a passing thought. This was God instructing me to be an example to the sheep.

I prayed, "Okay God, I'll find someone in the phonebook and write that person a letter. In fact, why don't You lay someone upon my heart to write?"

No sooner did I get this out of my mouth, than the name "Halston" came to me. I thought perhaps it was my own idea, so I tried to forget about it. But it came back for the second time–Halston. Then a third time, but this time there was a first name attached to it—"Michael Halston." I wondered if this could be the Holy Spirit speaking to me.

After hearing this name over and over again in my mind, I became convinced. When Debbie came out of the bank, I told her what had happened and that I thought God had given me this name. Debbie was used to my radical walk with God, and calmly agreed that it was probably God.

As soon as I got home, I reached for a phonebook, excited to see if there was a Michael Halston in there. Before I could get it opened, I heard the voice I was learning to become familiar with say, "Just remember, I am the same God who said you won't die of leukemia."

I threw down the phonebook. I didn't want to look because if the name "Michael Halston" wasn't there, then maybe I was really some kind of nut who heard voices and needed psychological care. Up until then, it was easy to preach and declare I had heard God, but this would be the proof. I slowly picked up the phonebook and turned to the "H's." Would there be such a name? After all, it wasn't the most common name in the world. As it turned out, there were five "Halstons" listed, and the very first name that appeared was "Michael Halston!"

That incident was just the beginning of God's words to me! They began to come to me in rapid-fire succession.

Approximately a week later, as I prepared to do some yard work at my mini-ranch in Springville, I called to the nearby city of Porterville to reserve a weed-eating tractor to use in my pasture. I picked up the tractor. It took three men to load it into my truck. With the tractor secured, I drove back to my mini-ranch, happy and carefree. I looked forward to spending a restful day working in the pasture. About halfway home, a rather alarming thought came to me. It had taken three guys to load up this tractor but I had no one to help me take it off the truck when I got home. What was I going to do? Needless to say, I found a way. When I arrived home, I rolled the tractor off the back of the truck, and dumped it onto my driveway. Then I happily mowed my weedy pasture. About thirty minutes into my plowing and disking, another thought came to me. *Hey, that tractor might have just rolled and bounced off of the truck, but it sure isn't going to roll and bounce back up into the truck.*

That thought passed through my mind, followed by the now familiar voice I'd come to recognize as the Holy Spirit's. He said, "I'm going to send someone to pick up your tractor for you, and you won't have to worry about getting it back up into the truck." Then, with emphasis, He added, "Just remember, I'm the one who has told you that you will not die of leukemia."

This time, I stopped what I was doing and laughed out loud. Apparently, He really wanted me to believe His promise. How He would pull this tractor thing off was beyond me, but this time I knew He would do it.

Sure enough, my father-in-law, who lived a few miles up the street, arrived at my house towing a special tractor-trailer behind his truck. He pulled into my driveway, rolled down his window and said, "I came by earlier and saw you out working on the tractor. Since I needed to go to Porterville today, I thought I'd load up your tractor in this trailer, and take it down there so you wouldn't have to mess with it."

God did it again. He gave me confirmation after confirmation. He continued to pound out His message to me. I was most definitely in the God-is-speaking-to-me zone.

I told Debbie, "If something happens now, and I do die of this disease I want a gravestone made that says, 'He died happy in Jesus, but he died confused.'" I was convinced God had given me a special message regarding my battle with leukemia. I believed He had led me into a radical lifestyle with Him so I could teach others about living by faith.

In Romans 10:17 it says that faith "comes from hearing, and hearing by the Word of Christ." "Word" is translated from the Greek, *rhema*—"a personal word that God speaks directly to the heart."

Many people today try to stir up faith in their own hearts, but without God's Word becoming personalized and a part of their lives, they won't have faith. People who hang around with God a lot, in prayer and fellowship, are usually filled with the faith they need to accomplish whatever He has for them to do. When David fought Goliath, most likely God had spoken some faith-filled words to his heart, for it is in the book of Psalms that we're told, "Thy Word I have treasured in my heart, that I may not sin against Thee" (119:11). The word "sin" basically means missing the mark or the target. God has many targets for us to hit in life, and the Greek word for "word" here can refer to a *rhema* spoken to our hearts, through a song, sermon, Bible passage, or any other means. When we hear God speak a word to us in a sermon, a song or from the Bible, we should meditate on it, hide it away in our heart, and keep it alive for the day we will need the faith to hit the target—accomplish the work God has for us. This is one reason why I encourage my congregation to keep their sermon notes tucked away somewhere where they can review them. This helps them keep a constant flow of God's faith in their hearts.

About a month passed and though God had fulfilled a promise to me, my body hadn't complied with the word I believed I had received. My blood remained unhealthy, plagued with the Philadelphia chromosome that causes leukemia, and I still had to undergo blood tests every other week. One of my doctors asked me if I was any more open to a bone marrow transplant than I had been previously. Time began to be a factor, and even though my chances of surviving such a procedure were not all that great, he thought a transplant might be my only option. But for me it wasn't an option because God Almighty had already spoken and told me that if I were to undergo this procedure, I would lose my life in the process.

That's what this book is all about. It's about listening for God and letting His Spirit navigate you through tough circumstances. I'm convinced that if we seek the Lord and godly counsel, and listen for the still, small voice in our hearts, God would save us from many of life's ordeals.

I once read about a man who had just won a handball championship game. What was unique about this man was that he only had one arm. When asked what made him such a great handball player, he responded, "Oh, that's quite simple. A handball game is primarily won or lost by how a person makes split-second decisions. One decision that most handball players have to make every second on the court is which hand they will use to make each corresponding shot. I don't have to make that decision. It's already made for me. So, I can respond to each shot sometimes quicker than others. That's what I believe makes me a good handball player."

In the same way, when God is at the helm and calling the shots, it makes life a lot easier. And I too can become a champion. The General of my life had already given me orders regarding a bone marrow transplant. Acknowledging and heeding His guidance makes life so much easier.

God wants to be in control of our health and our well-being. How many people would still be married today if they had only learned to sense the Holy Spirit's guidance during the heat of marital battle? Where would their lives be at today if they had heard God say, "Forgive." "Pray and be still." "Wait." "Get counsel." "Take authority over spirits."

How many people might still be alive if they had sensed God's leading them to forgo chemotherapy or, conversely, to accept chemotherapy? What if they had sensed God saying, "Change your diet." "Stop worrying." "Deal with the smoking or drinking habit now." "Go to the doctor for a physical." If only they had obeyed that ongoing voice of the Holy Spirit as He spoke through others, as well as in the inner recesses of their hearts.

How many kids would not be embittered toward their parents today or ever given over to drug habits or alcoholism if their ears had been trained to hear God's promptings? If they had only yielded themselves to the sermons that were spoken as a result of the Holy Spirit's anointing. If parents had taken more seriously the messages they heard on spending more time with their kids or on monitoring the friends that their kids hang out with, would that have made a difference?

Unfortunately, way too many Christians are too busy to listen—too busy to pray and too busy to obey. The devil wants us to be defeated in each and every area of our life. He knows that the only way to accomplish that is to prevent us from hearing God's voice. Jesus Himself said, "Man shall not live on bread alone, but on every word that proceeds out of the mouth of God" (Matthew 4:4). Either we believe that or we don't.

It became clear that it was God who guided every step, and it was a marvelous journey. Though my body refused to comply with the promises, I resolved to live by faith—the conviction and assurance of things I could not yet see. Isn't that what the Christian life is all about?

1. Charles Spurgeon, *Spurgeon's Sermons, Vol. 4* (Grand Rapids, MI: Baker Book House, 1983), 287.

# 7

## GREEN ACRES IS
## THE PLACE FOR ME

❖

*"A righteous man cares for the needs of his animal."*

—∽ PROVERBS 12:10A, NIV ∾—

During the challenges with my health, I made a move to the foot of the Sierras to a little town called Springville, California—population of about 1,500 people. I built a house with a perfect view of the snow-capped Sierras from my front porch. I've always had a desire to live on a little farm. So after building the home, I began to collect some animals. First, I bought a horse, and everything went pretty well. We occasionally rode her, and she added an ambiance to the property. Then came the cows. My wife warned me that I wasn't ready for any cows, simply because I hadn't checked out all the fencing in my pasture area. I reassured her that only after I got the cows would I be inspired to begin to work on the fence. She bought into it, and I wound up with some cows that didn't stay home a lot. I spent many nights herding cows from down the street or a neighbor's yard. This was real living to me, very therapeutic.

One day, Debbie commented that she really wanted a miniature pig—the kind that could be housebroken. I remembered that her aunt, who lived down in Porterville, raised these creatures. So I gave her a call and asked her if I might purchase one. She said that if I came over, she would just give me one. One day, when my daughter Tara and granddaughter Kylee were visiting, I decided to pay Debbie's aunt a visit and pick out a pig. Tara, Kylee and I jumped into my pickup truck and headed to town to "get us a pig." I was amazed when I saw the size of these "miniature pigs." Even the small ones were probably heavier than I could easily pick up. I also had a preconceived notion that these animals would be spotlessly clean, with perhaps a little bow around their necks. No such deal. I guess a pig that lives outdoors is a little different from a pig that shares a family's home.

Just then, I heard the bleating of some sheep and goats. "What's that?" I asked.

Debbie's aunt said those were the cries of some miniature goats. When I asked if I could have one of those instead of the pig, she said, "Sure, let's go pull one out!"

After we picked out a goat, my daughter drove the truck while I held the goat in my lap. Three-year-old Kylee sat in the middle. I just knew little Kylee would be thrilled, but I wasn't prepared for her response. Every time the goat bleated out one of his homesick cries, Kylee screamed and cried, and told me to take the goat back. She didn't like it.

I hoped she'd change her mind. Once we arrived home, I introduced the goat to a brand new pen I had built for it, with my father's help. The little goat stood in the middle of his new pen, and looked at the fence surrounding him. He pawed the dirt a couple of times, put his head down and charged the fence, striking it head-on with his little horns. The trauma of the sudden impact caused the goat to collapse to the ground. His body went into a spasm as blood trickled from of the corner of his mouth. My daughter, granddaughter and wife looked on in horror.

"What happened, Dad?"

"I don't know. I think he just broke his neck!"

Everyone stood there dazed as the poor animal lay on the ground, jerking and going into convulsions. To make things worse, they all turned to me, "Ronnie the Rancher," to see what I would do. I stood there for what seemed like an eternity and then turned to walk toward the house.

"Where are you going, Dad?"

"To get my gun and put that little critter out of his misery," I answered.

"Oh no! You can't do that! Oh, Dad, why not go in there and pray for him?" my daughter pleaded.

Pray for him? I never thought of that. Would it be sacrilegious to go into a pen and lay hands on a goat? I was on the spot, and knew I had to do something. So, into the pen I went. I knelt beside the goat, with my little band of parishioners looking on, and prayed, "God, please help this little goat, something is wrong with him. In Jesus' name, amen."

Amazingly, the little goat, within a matter of ten seconds, opened his eyes, struggled to his feet, shook his head two or three times, and seemed as normal as he was before all this happened. Oh, ye of little faith!

Somehow, we stray away from the simplicity of the gospel message. The Bible tells us to cast _all_ of our cares upon the Lord because He cares for us (ref. 1 Peter 5:7). Now, in my dictionary "all" means just that—_all!_ The Bible is written in such a way that everyone, with the help of the Holy Spirit, can draw great depths of wisdom from its pages. We just need to apply ourselves to the cause and put out a little effort.

Just as in fishing, praying involves a process. The bait a fisherman places in the net could represent our prayer requests and burdens. The fisherman casts the net out into the water. After a while, he pulls it back in to check it. He removes everything the sea has deposited. In our lives, this catch can symbolize words, comments or conversations God has with us during our prayer time.

The fisherman casts the net out into the deep once again. He does this over and over again until he receives the desired results.

I had a sick goat. So, I went to God, put my burden or care into the net, and cast it out into God's throne room. Then I waited for Him to respond. Likewise, we all can cast our nets into God's throne room. Once He responds, we obey what He's told us to do. If there's still a need there, we can cast our burden back in prayer again, and wait for further directions. I heard a preacher say one day that when you're looking for spiritual guidance, do what you know and then you'll know what to do. If you take "Step A," even if that's all you know to do, then and only then will God lead you to "Step B."

Actually, this is the process I used with my leukemia. I went to God with my burden and I cast it upon Him. I waited, and He began to speak. One of the responses He gave was, "Don't do a bone marrow transplant. Take Vitamin C. Deal with sin in your life." And I obeyed. Then I cast my burden back on Him and waited to see what else He would put in my net. I kept doing this until I got the desired results.

I cast today's cares upon God, and He gives me direction and grace for today. And for tomorrow's cares I'll do the same.

It's that simple. However, how many of us would have been "simple" enough to be like the people in the Bible? I doubt that many of us would have ever dreamed that God could use a young boy's slingshot to knock off a Philistine champion, giving him his first and last career loss. Who among us would have had childlike faith enough to listen to the voice of a donkey and seriously take his admonition? The point is, these people were not confined by what seems to be elementary rules of commonsense. According to 2 Kings 6:5-6, Elisha made an axe head float. Most of us would never even dream of asking God to do something so wildly bazaar! As I've said many times, "I live in God's experimental laboratory, and to me, kingdom life is an adventure. I try to make it as exciting as I can."

I remember one special time in my life when a parishioner in the church died suddenly of a massive heart attack. He was only fifty years old. In my mind, that was way too young to die and leave his wife. I went to the mortuary on a Monday morning to view the body. As I closed the door behind me, a wild thought entered my mind: *Here I am in an empty room with this dead person. Why not experiment and see if I can raise him from the dead. What will it hurt?*

I leaned close to Bert's ear and said, "Bert, in Jesus' name, I command you to get up! Get up, Bert! In Jesus' name!"

I repeated it three more times, each time increasing the volume and the authority of my command. Then I paced back and forth across the room, thanking God for the miracle He was about to do. I figured if I was going to experiment, I might as well experiment with some faith.

As I paced, I kept an eye on Bert. All of a sudden, I stopped dead in my tracks. I thought I saw Bert breathe. Could it be? What in the world would I tell the mortician lady at the front desk if I walked out of the room with Bert trailing behind me, straightening out the wrinkles on his suit as he followed? As it turned out, I didn't have to explain anything because Bert stayed dead. But the point is, what did it hurt to experiment a little?

In the story recorded in 2 Kings 4:18-37, it didn't look as if Elisha knew what he was doing when he raised the Shunammite's son from the dead. First he had his servant place a stick on the dead boy's face, but that didn't work. So Elisha tackled the problem himself. He paced and prayed a lot, and I think he may have been amazed when the boy sneezed and came back to life. I can tell you one thing for sure, Elisha wouldn't have revived that boy if he hadn't tried. And no one will perform any miracles if they don't at least try. I've even tried to walk on water. It didn't work, but perhaps someday I'll succeed, if it's God's will.

I like to have fun with my Christianity. In my opinion, there are way too many bored Christians who look as if they've been baptized in lemon juice. Their heralded message is: "Get saved and become like me—a bitter, old, bored coot."

"No, thank you!" is the unbelieving world's reply, and for good reason!

My recipe for maintaining "Christ appeal" calls for wholesome, but fun ingredients—savory lessons learned through life on my farm. The pond in front of our house began a sequence of events that led to another application of Scripture. As I gazed at the pond, on a quiet, fall morning, I decided I wanted some ducks. I checked the newspaper, and sure enough, I found some ducks for sale in Porterville, which is about twelve miles from my house. I proceeded to buy a couple of mallard ducks, a male and a female. I couldn't wait to put them in my pond. The guy who sold them to me assured me that they wouldn't run away. So into the pond they went. They stayed with me for months. They were very friendly ducks, especially the female. Daily I would go down to the pond and feed them some breadcrumbs, and they would usually meet me halfway in the pasture. They remained loyal to the family pond for quite a while, but after a few months, they became restless and wandered off. Usually they would only be gone for a couple of days at a time, and then they would come home. One day, after they had been gone for a couple of days, Debbie and I were out for our morning walk. When we spotted a couple of ducks a half a mile away from the house, I cried, "Those are my ducks!"

"How do you know they're your ducks?" Debbie asked. "All ducks look the same!"

"Believe me," I replied, "a farmer knows his ducks. Watch this!"

I called out to the ducks, and they lifted their heads and began to follow us home. Boy did I love this life!

After a while, the ducks disappeared for good and never came back again. Determined to have ducks again, I visited the feed store and bought two baby ducks. I purchased a little cage and brought them home. I raised them in my front room for months, to my family's chagrin. Boy, did the family ever complain! The kids would sit in the living room and try to eat dinner or watch TV, but they would start to gag. A permanent duck manure smell saturated our house. But that wasn't about to stop me. The ducks weren't big enough to be turned loose yet.

We endured the new ducks for a couple more weeks in the house, and then it came time to release them in the pond. I took them to their new home, opened their little pen and let them go. It was their first time in the big pond. My heart rejoiced to see them swim and enjoy their new home. Everything was fine for about ten minutes, and then they did the unexpected. They swam through a drainpipe that led over to the neighbor's pasture. From there they ran eastward, with me in hot pursuit. This couldn't be happening! These little guys were off to see a bigger and better world, and they never came home.

A few weeks later Kylee came to stay with us. An idea inspired me as we sat around the house one day. I said, "Kylee, how about you and I go down to the feed store in Porterville to buy some baby chicks?"

She liked my idea, so off we went. I decided that with my luck and lack of experience with raising baby chicks, I had better buy a lot because most of them would probably die. So I bought eighteen, and brought them home. I put them in a rabbit hutch. Then I bought a portable floodlight to keep them warm. As luck would have it, all eighteen lived and grew into big chickens. And now I had a big problem on my hands. I had way too many chickens. I drove around town and asked people if they wanted some chickens. Soon, I found a taker, and I gave them all away except for six hens and one rooster.

Now here's one of those "savory lessons" I learned from my chickens. I kept the six hens and one rooster in a large pen behind the house. One night, I heard the dog bark. Spotlight in hand, I looked into the pasture next door and I saw a pair of bright shining eyes about fifteen feet away from the chicken pen. Then I shined the light into the chicken pen and saw that my chickens were all sound asleep, perched up on the dowel rod I had put in there for them. Little did they know that imminent danger was nearby.

I often tell my congregation that the Bible says the devil is like a roaring lion that prowls around and seeks to devour its prey. Those chickens were only safe because of the pen I had built around them. If it hadn't been for the pen, they would have been dead meat.

We don't have to delve too deep to understand what this means for us. As we abide in God's Word and the fellowship of the Holy Spirit, God builds a protective hedge around us, and the devil can't get to us. But once we venture out from under God's protective covering, we're open prey. James once wrote: "But each one is tempted when he is carried away and enticed by his own lust. Then when lust has conceived, it brings forth death" (James 1:14-15). Satan is the tempter, and it is his job, along with his cohorts, the spirits of darkness, to tempt us to come out of the protective henhouse that God has prepared for us. And once we do, we become an easy target.

Let me explain it to you in yet another way. In 2 Corinthians 2:11 Paul writes that he has acted in a Christlike manner "in order that no advantage be taken of us by Satan; for we are not ignorant of his schemes." "Schemes" is translated from the Greek noema, which means: "a concept of the mind, a device, a contrivance." A scheme can include such things as evil ambushes.

The book of Joshua describes how the Israelites entered the Promised Land and conquered the heathen tribes who lived there. In chapter 6, they successfully knocked down the walls of Jericho and overcame the first obstacle to them possessing the land. Then in chapters 7 and 8, they ran into a roadblock at the city of Ai. They lost the battle there because of sin in the camp. The part I want to draw your attention to is in chapter 8 when God tells Joshua and the people that in order to win this battle, they had to ambush the people of Ai. Joshua did as he was commanded. He ordered 30,000 men to take their positions behind the city of Ai. Then he instructed 5,000 men to stand in front of the city in plain view. In this way, the men of Ai were lured to come out of their fortified city and give chase to what seemed to be an easy victory for them. When they stormed out of their fortified city to chase what they thought was the enemy, the larger army swept down on the city from the rear and destroyed it.

When we stay in God's fellowship with the Word, prayer and living holy lives, God puts a protective shield over us. According to 1 John, those who are strong in the Lord, who have His Word in their hearts, have "overcome the evil one" (2:14). But the devil has schemes and tricks. He wants to pull one over on us. He sets his ambushes, and tries to work them in much the same way as Joshua did his godly ambush. In order to lure us out of our fortified place, the devil dangles temptation of the flesh in front of us everyday—things that are forbidden by the Word of God, like sexual immorality, the lure of illicit drugs and alcohol, among others. Once we let the lure of these temptations get to us, and we leave the protective covering of God's grace to pursue them, the enemies of darkness can invade our homes, church lives, and our marriages. The enemy's intentions are to destroy our place of fortification. And sometimes, while we're out there pursuing the sins of the flesh, the devil destroys our fortified place to such a degree that we sometimes cannot go back there. Many Christian men, especially, have been duped into one of these ambushes. They grow careless with their daily devotions and prayer. They regularly start missing some church services, and before they know it, they're stuck in a sinful situation. We have been genetically coded with sin from the day Adam sinned in the Garden of Eden, and now we have a sickness in our flesh that must be kept in remission by a consistent diet of the Word, prayer and fellowship. If we ever get away from this spiritual medicine, our disease will take over again. For example, some men unfortunately get caught up in immorality, and the devil comes in from the blindside and informs the wife of the adulterous affair or the drug use or whatever may be the case. All of a sudden, the man can't go home, to the place of protection anymore. Sometimes he's even ashamed to go back to church because everyone knows about his infidelities. Slowly he's picked apart pretty much like what a wild animal would do to a chicken that had ventured out of the chicken coop. This is the nature of an ambush!

The devil is always close by, but because of the protective hedge God has put around us, we may not be aware of it. Just like those chickens, danger is just a step away. And we as Christians should take heed lest we become negligent and fall into the enemy's trap.

Just remember, an immoral affair doesn't start out as an immoral affair. It's the beginning point. It may be negligence in our personal lives, which leads to negligence in our church attendance. Then it's on to our television and Internet habits, and soon it's a casual fantasizing about the secretary at work. It's all a contrived, well thought-through plan of the enemy to lure us out of the henhouse so he can destroy us.

Debbie once told me, "The steps leading up to an immoral affair are like the descending steps leading down a staircase. With each step, you have a chance to stop, turn around and go back to your original place." It's my prayer that we always remain in the chicken coop and enjoy the life that God has prepared for us.

It was a healing time on the farm—a therapeutic time that God had set aside for me. It lasted a short three years, but it was a season of life with purpose. And once the purpose had been accomplished, I had to move on. I still had my leukemia, but God had a plan.

# 8

# THE MAGIC PILL AND GOD'S HEALING TOUCH

❖

*"Ultimate healing and the glorification of the body are certainly among the blessings of Calvary for the believing Christian. Immediate healing is not guaranteed. God can heal any disease, but He's not obligated to do so."*

—⌒ WARREN WIERSBE[1] ⌒—

*"Because we are the handiwork of God, it follows that all our problems and their solutions are theological."*

—⌒ A.W. TOZER[2] ⌒—

On March 19, 1998, I was told about a clinical trial that would be conducted at UCLA. A pill that had been developed and researched in an Oregon laboratory had produced some significant results with rats that had Chronic Myelogenous Leukemia (CML). According to my doctor, this pill could be the "silver bullet" for this type of leukemia. Without hesitation, I volunteered to be part of the clinical trial. I felt at peace about this decision.

Three months later, on June 22, I became the first person in the world to take this trial pill called "STI-571", now known as "Gleevec." The doctors and nurses gave me a 25-milligram pill, while an audience from Europe listened in via a telephone conference call. Everyone applauded when I downed the pill with an eight-ounce glass of water. Going into the trial, I was somewhat concerned because of the way trials are run. I knew that the first few patients would get a 25-milligram pill, and they would remain on that dosage for three months. After three months, if it didn't work, these people would leave the trial program, return to their former drugs, and a new test group would be administered a higher dosage. People would revolve in and out until they found a dosage that worked. In my mind, we were like guinea pigs, and I was acutely aware of the fact that no one thought a low dosage of 25 milligrams would actually do anything. They didn't expect the pill to work until the dosage increased to around 200-300 milligrams.

I began to think that being one of the first people in the trial was a curse, because once the pill failed, it might be years before the FDA approved it, and I could be dead by then! But I talked to God a lot about it. He spoke to my spirit one day and told me something very liberating. He said, "It doesn't matter if you take 25 milligrams or 525, your life is in *My* hands, and *I'll* say when and if you die." So, I went in and kicked off the experiment with a heart of confidence and expectancy, knowing that God was totally in control.

The pill didn't work at 25 milligrams. I rotated out of the clinical trial, and resumed taking conventional medicine. According to the medical field, my time clock was ticking. It had been almost two years since my initial diagnosis. The average life expectancy was three to four years. I reminded myself that God had a plan; that He had told me I would not die of CML. But whatever He was going to do, I wished He would hurry and do it. I hated living with the suspense.

In the interim, God's people continued to encourage me with words from God, many of which I believed were right on. Many had to do with demon spirits and angels. Three interesting episodes concerning demon spirits had already occurred. On three separate occasions, during my diagnostic period, I experienced a fever accompanied by chills and aches that I associated with the leukemia. On each occasion, after a ten-minute radical engagement in spiritual warfare, all of the symptoms disappeared as quickly as they came. This led me to believe that there had to be some link to the demonic realm involved. Many more things happened to me that encouraged my belief that my leukemia was tied to the demonic realm. According to my wife's and my calculations, I contracted leukemia during a period of time when I had engaged in fervent prayer for a lady in our church that was dying of cancer. Debbie and I visited the woman and her husband at their home, one night, to pray for them. I believe she had lymphoma, and the doctors had not given her long to live. As we sat and conversed, I asked her about some of her symptoms. She told me of her swollen lymph glands and her sheet-drenching night sweats. Before the night ended, we all stood in the middle of the woman's living room and prayed. In the course of the prayer that night, I felt led to take authority over the spirits of cancer and disease. As I did, we were startled to hear a crashing, thumping sound on the sliding glass doors behind us. The sound caused their dogs in the backyard to rush toward the doors, barking in a frenzy.

During the pause in our prayers, the woman commented that she felt something take place in her body as I prayed. We never did identify what made the noise. But on that particular night, I went home and, for the first time in my entire life except for a couple of occasions when I had the flu, I woke up twice to change my sweat-soaked T-shirt. That incident caused me to consider the possibility of there being some sort of demonic link. Although I have no biblical reference to quote for the possibility of the following idea to be true in the world today, I still have to wonder if it didn't play a role in the demonic part of my trial. There is a group of people near our city who claim to be a coven of witches. Their leader is pretty well known in our town. After being diagnosed over a year, one of our leader's wives approached me after a service and told me that the leader of the witches' coven had approached her at work and had asked her how I was doing health wise. She said, "Oh, our pastor is doing wonderful! He couldn't be better. Why do you ask?"

And with a smirk on his face, he told her, "We have been praying for his death for some time now. We feel that if he should die, Valley Bible Fellowship would be much less of a success in our city."

This whole idea brought up many questions in my mind, such as, *Is it possible for people to pray to Satan, and if so, how much influence in the demonic realm can these prayers have?* Was it just a coincidence that they had been praying and I was sick, or was it slightly possible that maybe I needed to be educated more on the demonic realm and how it worked? Obviously, by his response, he thought their prayers were working, and we do know that the magicians and sorcerers of Pharaoh's court in the Old Testament had some sort of powers granted to them from Satan. In fact, some of these signs closely resembled the signs and miracles sent from the hands of God. I also know that in the Bible some illnesses are demonically induced. So this idea just added to my wondering if some of my problems with my health could be related to the other realm.

Some years previous to this encounter, while I conducted a demonic deliverance, a demon vowed to kill me someday. Theologically I tried to categorize my illness. I knew the Bible explicitly related occasions when evil spirits caused sickness to come upon certain individuals. For example, in Luke 13:10-11, we are told of a woman who, for eighteen years, had had a sickness *caused by a spirit.* In verse 16, Jesus says of her "and this woman, a daughter of Abraham as she is, whom Satan has bound for eighteen long years." Many times in Scripture Jesus tells of healing people who were sick because of demons. My intentions are not to make a doctrinal case out of this, but just to explore the possibilities.

I believe we already know some of the reasons for many illnesses today. They can be caused by the environment, bad eating habits, worry, stress, cigarette smoke and alcohol consumption, the sun's rays, to name a few. And perhaps demon spirits cause some remote illnesses.

I'll never forget praying for a very young blind child, many years ago. As I prayed, a consuming desire to take authority over spirits came over me. As I began to do so, with the young child in my arms, I distinctly felt a set of teeth sink into my chest when I mentioned demons. The child had bitten down on my chest, and with each denunciation of demons, the clench became tighter until I could bear the pain no longer. I have no explanation for manifestations like that. But I do know that the Apostle Paul warned us that our battle in this world was primarily against spirits without bodies (ref. Ephesians 6:12). I've done enough deliverances to know that demons truly exist in our world. They are a lot more active than we give them credit for being.

Regarding my leukemia, God through His people, stressed

the importance of believing and daily quoting the Word aloud. So, on my daily prayer walks, I shouted out verses like the one God had given me as a promise—Psalm 91:7-8a: "A thousand may fall at [my] side, and ten thousand at [my] right hand; but it shall not approach [me]. [I] will only look on with [my] eyes" (bracketed personalizations, mine).

One of my favorite verses I quoted daily was Psalm 118:17, "I shall not die, but live and tell of the works of the Lord." I quoted the Word often with great zeal and boldness, and I felt so much better when I did. God had a plan, but I needed to walk in faith.

We don't walk in faith very often. Walking in faith is simply living as if the promises God has given us are already locked in place. The Apostle Paul quoted Habakkuk 2:4 when he reminded the believers in Rome that the "righteous man shall *live by faith*" (Romans 1:17, italics mine). I didn't want to wait until I had been healed to praise God; I wanted to praise Him before the fact. I wanted people to see the authenticity of God.

I ran into a friend at the supermarket one day. She asked how I was doing. I told her that my blood count was going wild and that the medical field didn't give me much hope. "But," I told her, "God told me emphatically that I won't die because of this disease."

She looked at me and said, "I hope you're right! We need to see a miracle in this town."

Right there on the spot I made a deal with her that if I were still alive after five years, she would start coming to church. I bragged to everyone that God had told me I wouldn't die. I said that if they didn't believe me, all they had to do was hide and watch. I invited all the skeptics to pretend they were at the movies, grab some popcorn, and sit and watch. I told them that if I died of this disease, then perhaps my whole life was a sham and a fake. If so, they didn't need to take anything I had ever said too seriously. But on the other hand, if I did beat this thing, then it might behoove them to listen more closely to what I professed was from God.

One day, as Debbie and I drove to the mini-ranch in Springville from Bakersfield, I felt a stirring need to have someone who really knew how to pray lay hands on me. Lots of people had prayed for me, and I totally appreciated it, but I needed aggressive, radical prayer. I shun the "emotionalism thing" in the church today. There's a big difference between emotional prayer and aggressive radical prayer. I felt strongly that I needed someone to come against the leukemia—someone who had experience in radical healing prayer. When I shared this with Debbie, she reminded me of a pastor in town by the name of Glen Brown. This wasn't the first time she had suggested him. He definitely was radical—perhaps more so than I desired. I continued to decline her recommendation. So, I said, "Let's just let God lay a person upon our heart, because He knows exactly who to have pray for me."

We prayed and played what I call the "Ronnie Game." I asked her, "Did God lay anyone upon your heart?"

And she said, "He sure did—Glen Brown."

"Boy, you sound like a broken record," I commented.

"What about you, Ron?" she asked.

"An old friend came into my mind out of the clear blue sky, Steve Harp."

I hadn't seen Steve or his wife Teresa for a long time, but I made up my mind to call him. Well, I never got the chance to call Steve because out of the blue, Steve called me the next

day! He told me I had been on his heart and that he was praying for me.

I explained that God had put him upon my heart the day
before. This couldn't be a coincidence.

When he invited me to his church's prayer meeting the
following Thursday night, I thought, *Why not?* I accepted his
invitation and asked, "Where do you go to church?"

"Glen Brown's."

Was God in control or what? When I told my wife, she
just looked at me with a silly grin on her face. I hate it when
my wife gets on a roll like this. It seemed as though she had
a better hotline to God than I had. It was becoming very
humbling!

When Thursday arrived, I had a blood test during the
day. My white blood cell count was 25,000—more than twice
what it was supposed to be. Usually, when it was this high,
the doctor would increase my medicine. In a week or two,
my blood count would come down slowly but surely. But it
never came down without an increase in medicine.

That evening, Debbie and I, and my 25,000 white blood
count went to a prayer meeting at this little Pentecostal
church across town. When we arrived, there were probably
thirty people inside praying with the lights turned down low.
Some paced back and forth in the front of the church down
by the altar; some knelt and others stood facing the walls. I
sat in the back with Debbie, and quietly prayed while we
waited for them to acknowledge our presence. After about
thirty minutes or so, Glen Brown asked us to come up front
so they could pray for me. They all gathered around us and,
with Pastor Glen Brown leading the prayer, they laid hands
on me. With one hand on my forehead, Pastor Glen raised his

voice and commanded every demon of hell to let loose of God's son, and he then commanded leukemia to leave my body. He said a lot of other things I can't remember, but what I do remember is that when I left, I felt really prayed for. I knew that if God was ever going to show up at a prayer meeting, He showed up at that one.

The following Monday, I had my blood checked. I couldn't believe my eyes! Without any increase in medication, my blood count had gone back to a normal 7.5. When I told my nurses what had happened, they were flabbergasted. Now, here's the clincher. The following day, I was called back by UCLA and told that because I was gracious enough to be the first person in the world to start off the STI-571 clinical trial, they wanted me to come back into the trial at a higher dosage of 300 milligrams. However, before I could begin the trial, I needed to eliminate all medication and let my white blood cell count go up to a higher range so they could measure the effects of STI-571. I fully complied the next day. Never before had I dared to go off my medication for any length of time because I knew that in just a matter of days, my white blood cell count would skyrocket. Usually without medication, it would sometimes go up 3,000 - 5,000 a day. But this time I was in for a surprise. After Glen had prayed for me, my white blood cell count refused to go up. For one whole week it remained normal, then two weeks, and then three weeks. What was I going to do? Now for the first time in my life I wanted it to go up and it wouldn't. The nurses even admitted that they had never seen anything quite like it before.

Meanwhile, UCLA got tired of waiting for my white blood cell count to go up, so they gave me the pill and said to start taking it. As anxious as I had been before to get on these pills at that dose, I wanted to first wait and see if I was healed before I started on any medication. I waited four weeks, five weeks, and still my white blood cell count remained normal. What would I do? I was in a dilemma because UCLA thought I had already been on the pill for two weeks, but I hadn't taken the first pill yet. If I refused to take them, then they would probably kick me out of the trial. Then if my blood did decide to go back up, I would be out of the trial and back on drugs that could only help temporarily.

Every day, my wife and I walked and prayed. I agonized over what I should do. Finally one day, Debbie spoke some words of life to me, when she told me that I was making too big of a deal out of it. She told me that no matter which decision I made, God would understand. I felt obligated, at that point, to prove a healing for God, so He would get the glory, if in fact one did exist. I felt pressured to be God's trophy, and I'm not so sure He was the one pressuring me. I began to worry about what people would think if I went on the pill. Would they say that I lacked faith? Even some of the nurses in Bakersfield didn't want me to take the pill because they truly thought I was healed. I felt pressured by God. And although everyone else had his or her own opinion, it was my life. I needed to do what I thought was best, so I finally decided to start taking the medication, although my white blood cell count never left the normal ranges after that prayer meeting.

I believe I made the right decision to resume taking the pill. In the body of a person who has CML, a chromosome exists called the "Philadelphia chromosome." People without CML don't have this chromosome in their body. When a person goes into remission, the white blood cell count stabilizes even without medication sometimes, but the proof is in a procedure called a bone marrow biopsy. If, after the biopsy is performed, the presence of the Philadelphia chromosome is still present, and the disease is still there, then more than likely, the white blood cell count will race out of control sooner or later.

After the prayer meeting, they did a bone marrow biopsy on me. Out of twenty samples of chromosomes they took out of my body, all tested positive with the Philadelphia chromosome. I still had the full-blown disease in my body. I made the right decision because when God does a miracle, it can stand any test or scrutiny. So what do I think happened at that prayer meeting? I believe in what the Bible says in James 5:16b that the fervent prayer of a righteous person accomplishes much. I credit the prayers of those people at Glen Brown's church as being the force that drove the leukemia into remission and perhaps generated a total healing.

Regardless of whether it was the result of prayer, the pill or a combination of both, here I am in June 2002, not only in a state of remission, but with all Philadelphia chromosomes gone. I'm one of the few that has entered uncharted territory with CML. Am I cured? The doctors won't say so yet because only time will tell, but two things I do know: (1) I'm not dying and (2) people are beginning to believe that God really did speak to me, and that if I hadn't listened to His voice every step along the way I would be dead today.

1. Warren W. Wiersbe, *Why Us?* (Old Tappan NJ: Fleming H. Revell, (1984) 152.

2. A.W. Tozer, *The Knowledge of the Holy* (New York: Harper & Row Publishers, (1961) 34.

# 9

# FOUR THINGS I'VE LEARNED SINCE I THOUGHT I KNEW IT ALL

❖

*"Because the foolishness of God is wiser than men,*
*and the weakness of God is stronger than men"*

—❦ 1 CORINTHIANS 1:25 ❧—

L et me leave you with four life lessons I've learned since I thought I knew it all:

## LIFE LESSON 1

I've learned through my recent ordeal just how easy it is to deal with little sins in your life when you know you have to. For me, when I was diagnosed with CML, I had a few compromising sins that I figured I had to live with because, after all, I was only human. Ever hear that justification? But once I thought it was quite possible that I might be seeing God sooner than later, you wouldn't believe how manageable those sins became.

I believe we've bought into a lie the devil has fabricated. The lie convinces us that we have no choice but to learn to live with certain little sins in our lives. In reality God expects us to live in complete holiness to the very best of our capability.

If you're having a hard time dealing with certain sins in your life, let me remind you of a story found in 1 Samuel 5. The Children of Israel were in a war with the Philistines. In the course of the battle, the tide turned in favor of the Philistines. They were even able to steal the Ark of the Covenant from the people of God. They took it home to Ashdad, and stored it away in the temple of their god Dagon. And when the priest of Dagon went out the next day to pay honor to their god, they were in for a surprise. Dagon had fallen over on his face to the ground. So they helped their god back up, thinking it was probably just a strange coincidence. Well, the next morning, when they went out to pay homage to Dagon, they noticed that not only had he fallen to the ground again, but this time when he fell, his head and hands broke off. Only his trunk was left. He was, you might say, broken to a point beyond repair. Now the point is plain and simple—Dagon can't stand in the presence of God's Spirit. The different sins in your life represent Dagons. And as you bring the presence of God into your life through praise music, fellowship, faithful church attendance, prayer, and memorization and quoting of the Word, your Dagons will not be able to stand. Let God arise and His enemies be scattered. Exalt God instead of waging war against the sin. Where He increases, sin will decrease.

## LIFE LESSON 2

Learn to acknowledge God in all of your ways and He will make your paths straight (Proverbs 3:6). I believe with all my heart that God speaks to us a lot more today than we think. But we're not listening to or acknowledging His voice. I'm convinced that had I not trained my ears to hear God, I would be dead today. First of all, I would have undergone a bone marrow transplant and not survived it because He told me I wouldn't have survived it. Second, had I stayed on chemotherapy treatments I may have irreparably harmed my immune system. God knows what's best for each individual; however, we can't apply to others what God specifically instructs for us to do. Each person must learn to hear God speak to him or her personally. For someone else, chemotherapy might be something God wants to use to heal that person. For another, a bone marrow transplant might be the winning ticket. Each one of us will have to travel our own life roads, so it's imperative that we each learn how to commune with God and learn how to sense His personal guidance and hear His voice in our lives.

## LIFE LESSON 3

God sees every little thing that I do and hears everything I say. Psalm 139:3 tells us God is intimately acquainted with all of our ways. In the past few years, God has supernaturally talked to me of matters about which I didn't know He was aware of.

More than twenty years ago, I went through a discouraging time in the ministry. I thought I should quit the ministry and divorce my wife. My burnout left me feeling apathetic about life, so I packed my bags and headed off to LA to party. After I checked in to a motel, I went to my car to unload my belongings. But when I opened the trunk, everything I'd packed was gone. It had literally disappeared. Gone was my suitcase, my spare money—even my Bible (although I wasn't sure why I had brought that along).

Then I heard a voice say, "This isn't anything compared to what you're going to lose if you don't pull yourself together right now."

I went back to my room in a daze. I still didn't get it, so I prayed, "God, please speak to me."

I reached into the motel drawer and pulled out a Gideon Bible. I randomly opened it and began to read: "Therefore you are without excuse, every man of you who passes judgment, for in that you judge another, you condemn yourself; for you who judge practice the same things. And we know that the judgment of God rightly falls upon those who practice such things" (Romans 2:1-2).

Needless to say, I went home with a new appreciation for how close God is to us every moment of the day, and how He sees it all and hears it all. Since that time, God has talked to me about some very personal issues—things I had no idea whatsoever he noticed. He sees every TV program we watch. He sees the way we treat others. He even knows our thoughts. He sees and He cares. And I believe He rewards us accordingly.

## LIFE LESSON 4

Most Christians basically misunderstand God's ways. God resides in the spirit realm. And, of course, we reside in the physical realm. Most of God's works come through the spirit realm. For example, when we pray for a financial raise on the job, and it's God's will that we have one, God begins to move upon the heart of our employer. And we eventually get a raise. Sometimes we wrongly proclaim we received a miracle when, in fact, God just did the kind of stuff He normally does in the spirit realm.

Or as another example, when we pray for a girlfriend or a boyfriend, and all of sudden someone falls madly in love with us, it's because God's Spirit moved upon them as we prayed. We may think it's a miracle, but it's most likely God moving in His normal way.

When it comes to physical healings, it's much the same thing! We get sick usually because of a specific reason—maybe we smoked and we got cancer, or we developed heart disease because we ate a lot of fatty foods and didn't exercise. Perhaps the disease is a result of excessive worry that wears down our body. Or we succumb to illness as a result of trying to live in sin and live for God at the same time.

When we get in the prayer lines at church, all we think about is "God, help me get rid of my illness!" Perhaps a sincere prayer warrior rebukes the cancer, the heart disease or whatever, but God knows that even if He performed a miracle and got rid of the illness, the illness would return if the person persisted in his or her sinful lifestyle.

This is the thought behind the text in James 5:13-16, where it says, "Is anyone among you suffering? Let him pray. Is anyone cheerful? Let him sing praises. Is anyone among you sick? Let him call for the elders of the church, and let them pray over him, anointing him with oil in the name of the Lord; and the prayer offered in faith will restore the one who is sick, and the Lord will raise him up, and if he has committed sins, they will be forgiven him. Therefore, confess your sins to one another, and pray for one another, so that you may be healed. The effective prayer of a righteous man can accomplish much."

Notice that the Greek word for "sick" in James 5:15 is the word *kamno*. It's only used two other times in Scripture—once in Hebrews 12:3 where it speaks of not "growing weary" and then in Revelation 2:3 where the Lord speaks to the church in Ephesus and tells them that although they've been through a lot, they've persevered and endured for His name's sake, "and have not grown weary." Basically *kamno* means "to be feeble, weary or worn out; to be dried up."

Quite possibly we sometimes need God to touch us in our spirit before He can do a work in our body. In fact, this text seems to indicate that there may be times when unconfessed sin could be responsible for our illnesses. The text encourages us to confess our sins and repent of them so we might be healed. As I said in chapter 4, God has designed our bodies in such a way that they try to heal themselves. And sometimes, if we remove the sin, the body will spring back to life. But unfortunately, in some situations, it's broken beyond its ability to repair itself, and that's when we have to ask God for a miraculous healing.

God made our bodies, and although healthcare professionals may not know of a cure for what ails us, that doesn't mean one doesn't exist.

For example, God's remedy may consist of rest and a daily dose of some basic herbs or vitamins; however, researchers haven't discovered that regimen yet. Through prayer, God can reveal His "prescription" via a book, a friend or through the one praying for us. As a result, we're healed. We may cry out "miracle!" when, in fact, it was God using natural means to accomplish the job. In this case, God reaches down from His spirit realm and uses the things in our physical realm to bring about natural healing.

James 5:17-18 says, "Elijah was a man with a *nature* like ours, and he prayed *earnestly* that it might not rain; and it did not rain on the earth for three years and six months. And he prayed again, and the sky poured rain, and the earth produced its fruit" (italics mine). This illustration puts a word picture in our minds of someone coming to the church for prayer. This person's life is all dried up and parched. As a result, no fruit grows in his life. He has no joy, and he is not motivated at all to bring the good news of the gospel to other people. He isn't producing any disciples. In his spirit he is depressed, discouraged and all dried up (spiritually speaking) because of sin. The Holy Spirit is grieved. But once the sin is confessed, and righteous people offer intercessory prayer, the obstacle for healing is removed, and the joy of the Lord returns. The Bible says the joy of the Lord is our strength (ref. Nehemiah 8:10).

This is one reason for us to stress that people who pray be people who stand rightly before God—people who are sensitive to how and what they pray, who have an ability to give forth words of prophecy, wisdom and knowledge.

Sometimes demon spirits can be involved with an illness, and it's critical that the people doing the praying pick up on this. How many of us have left our prayer lines more defeated than before we came, feeling unloved by God because He didn't meet our needs. Had the people praying for us picked up on what was going on in the spirit realm, and taken authority over demons, or possibly given us a word from God about diet or taking vitamins, things might have been different for us. We might have left feeling more renewed in our spirits and our bodies. I pray that people who are called to pray for others will see the seriousness of their calling. We are God's physicians, ministering to the whole man or woman. God might instruct us to tell someone to go home and sleep for eight hours, or He might lay upon our heart the desire to tell someone they need to forgive someone else for something they did to them, because an unforgiving heart can wreak havoc on our bodies. Sometimes when I pray for others, God leads me to recommend a health video to them, one that speaks a lot about diet and vitamins and taking care of the body. Yet at other times I just call out for God to do a miracle in someone's life. The secret is, I must be filled with the Holy Spirit when I pray for others, and I must not be careless in what I pray or be indifferent to what I feel the Holy Spirit is speaking to my heart. Now granted there are some diseases and illnesses that have nothing to do with sin, nor are they a result of a bad diet or an unforgiving heart. They may be genetic in nature, or perhaps the body has been poisoned or an organ is worn out. In such cases, we sometimes call upon God to move outside of His normal spiritual working place, and provide us with a miracle.

God does perform miracles today, so we must boldly and unashamedly ask for them. When He performs miracles, and why He performs them goes beyond our understanding. But any time He comes out of the spirit realm, moves and touches the physical realm and alters its reality with laws unknown to man and angels, we call that a miracle. And a miracle-working God He has always been and always will be.

In conclusion, there's always hope for you no matter what condition you're in—either physically, emotionally or relationally. I love to serve God and live for Him daily. It's truly an adventure and a wonderful way to live. No matter what my future holds for me, I proclaim loudly and boldly that we serve a good and gracious God. We must not be rendered useless in the Kingdom of God and the world by Satan's conspiracy to keep us in the dark regarding spiritual matters. We must begin to expend some effort to listen for God's voice and to look for His hand in our daily affairs.

I am very concerned that there are what I call too many "non-believing believers" in the world today. We say we believe in demons and angels, but then order our lives in such a way that our actions speak louder than our words. We never speak to demons or exercise our spiritual authority over them, nor do we ever expect angels to show up and help us.

We *say* we believe in the Word of God, but fail to spend much time studying it. Most Christians are biblically illiterate. We say we believe in evangelism, but rarely do we open our mouths to evangelize. Obviously we don't believe too much in heaven or hell or we would seriously be giving ourselves to the cause. We say that we firmly believe in God's grace and forgiveness, but we treat errant Christians much differently than we do those who we believe to be more righteous.

It is my hope that this book will call each and every one of us back to the Word of God, and that it will cause us to re-evaluate its message and quite possibly force us to redefine Christianity from what we thought it was to what it really is. It is my opinion that all the demons of hell are committed to keeping us in the dark lest the light of God should come through us and destroy the devil's kingdom. The way to life, victory and success is so simple that most of us miss it, because after all, there is a conspiracy to keep us locked up in a dark and silent world where God never enters.